THE YOUNGEST
STORYBOOK

By the same author
A STORYTELLER'S CHOICE
A SECOND STORYTELLER'S CHOICE

The Youngest Storybook

A Collection of Stories & Rhymes
for the Youngest

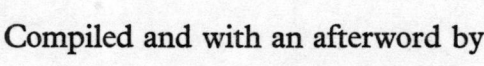

Compiled and with an afterword by
EILEEN COLWELL

Illustrated by
MARGERY GILL

THE BODLEY HEAD
LONDON · SYDNEY · TORONTO

All rights reserved
This collection © The Bodley Head Ltd, 1967
Illustrations © The Bodley Head Ltd, 1967
Printed and bound in Great Britain for
The Bodley Head Ltd
9 Bow Street, London, WC2
by C. Tinling & Co Ltd., Liverpool, London & Prescot
Set in Monotype Plantin
First published 1967

Acknowledgments

EVERY effort has been made to trace the ownership of the copyright material in this book. It is the publishers' belief that the necessary permissions from publishers, authors and authorised agents have been obtained, but in the event of any question arising as to the use of any material, the publishers, while expressing regret for any error unconsciously made, will be pleased to make the necessary correction in future editions of this book.

Thanks are due to the following for permission to reprint copyright material: Brockhampton Press Ltd for 'The Sleepy-Mouse' from *Lollipops* by Leila Berg; The Bodley Head Ltd, London and Doubleday & Company Inc., New York for 'The Picnic Basket' from *The Poppy Seed Cakes* by Margery Clark; Hutchinson & Co. Ltd, London and Ivan Obolensky, Inc., New York for 'Mr Puffblow's Hat' from *Little Old Mrs Pepperpot* by Alf Prøysen, translated by Marianne Helweg; Copyright 1959 by Alf Prøysen; The Society of Authors as the literary representative of the Estate of the late Rose Fyleman and Doubleday & Company Inc., New York for 'Mice' from *Fifty-one New Nursery Rhymes* by Rose Fyleman, Copyright 1932 by Doubleday & Company, Inc.; George G. Harrap & Sons Ltd for 'Teddy Robinson is a Red Indian' from *Teddy Robinson* by Joan G. Robinson; Evans Brothers Limited for 'Honey Bear' from *Book of 1000 Poems* by Elizabeth Lang; Faber and Faber Ltd for 'The Silver Thimble' from *Meet Mary Kate* by Helen Morgan;

The Bodley Head Ltd for 'The Tree Trick' from *A Hat for Rhinoceros* by Anita Hewett; The Bodley Head Ltd, London and McGraw-Hill Book Company Inc., New York for 'Jacko and the Potato Scones' from *Jacko and Other Stories* by Jean Sutcliffe, Copyright © 1964 by Jean Sutcliffe; Abelard-Schuman Limited for 'The Marriage of the Robin and the Wren' from *Twenty-Five Fables* by Norah Montgomerie; Basil Blackwell for 'The Dog and the Cock' from *Picture Tales from the Russian*, illustrated by Valery Carrick; The Author for 'J for John' and 'A Spring Story' by Vera Colwell, Copyright © 1967 Vera Colwell; A. & C. Black Ltd for 'The Engine Driver' and 'Marching in our Wellingtons' from *Speech Rhymes*, edited by Clive Sansom; Faber and Faber Ltd for 'Tim Rabbit's Sneeze' from *Adventures of Tim Rabbit* by Alison Uttley; Jonathan Cape Ltd, Mrs H. M. Davies and Wesleyan University Press, Connecticut for 'The Rain' from *The Complete Poems of W. H. Davies*, Copyright © 1963 by Jonathan Cape Ltd; Miss Marjorie Poppleton for 'The Little Yellow Comb' from *Ten Tales for the Very Young* by Marjorie Poppleton, published by the University of London Press; Miss Ann Wolfe for 'The Blackbird' by Humbert Wolfe; Mrs Lilian Daykin for 'The Little Woman's Water-Pot', Copyright © 1967 Lilian Daykin. Miss Catherine Woolley for 'A Garage for Gabriel' from *Read Me Another Story*, published by Thomas Y. Crowell Company, New York; Mrs Joan Rodney Bennett for 'Safety First' from *Adventures in Words*, published by the University of London Press; Brockhampton Press Ltd for 'The Little Brown Egg' from *Lollipops* by Leila Berg; William Heinemann Ltd for 'Charles and Jenny' from *Listen with Mother Tales* by Ruth Ainsworth; Faber and Faber Ltd for 'The Pretty Little Hen and Bad Mr Wolf' from *Nursery Tales* by Diana Ross; Faber and Faber Ltd for 'Blackie's Birthday' from *A Story A Day* by Doris Rust; Faber and Faber Ltd for 'Henrietta and The Cows' from *The Adventures of*

Henrietta Hen by Aaron Judah; George G. Harrap & Sons Ltd and Hughes Massie Ltd for 'Galldora and the Rooks' from *The New Adventures of Galldora* by Modwena Sedgwick; The Bodley Head Ltd for 'Elephant Big and Elephant Little' from *Elephant Big and Elephant Little* by Anita Hewett; Faber and Faber Ltd for 'Jane and the Hair Wave' from *Stories for Jane* by Catherine Storr; Methuen & Co. Ltd, London and W. W. Norton & Co., Inc., New York for 'Puss and Pup' from *Harum Scarum* by Josef Căpek, translated by Stephen Jolly; J. Garnet Miller Ltd for 'Cuckoo' from *A Story to Tell* by Barbara Ker Wilson; Oxford University Press Ltd, London and E. P. Dutton & Co. Inc., New York for 'The Magic Seeds' from *The Blackbird in the Lilac* by James Reeves; Methuen & Co. Ltd and Mr Donald Bisset for 'Honk Honk' from *Another Time Stories* by Donald Bisset; Angus & Robertson Ltd for 'The Old Red Bus' from *Listening Time* by Jean Chapman; Lansdowne Press, Melbourne for 'About Mr MacPherson's Ducks' from *Storytime* by Marjorie Cleine; David Higham Associates Ltd for 'Mrs Peck Pigeon' and 'Good-night' from *Silver Sand and Snow* by Eleanor Farjeon, published by Michael Joseph Ltd; Harcourt, Brace & World, Inc. for 'If you Find a Little Feather' from *Something Special* by Beatrice Schenk de Regniers, Copyright © 1958 by Beatrice Schenk de Regniers; Brockhampton Press Ltd for 'All Change!' from *Country Bunch* by Ursula Hourihane; Faber and Faber Ltd for 'The Little Fir-Tree' from *The Weathercock* by Alison Uttley.

Contents

Acknowledgments, 5
The Sleepy-Mouse, *Leila Berg*, 11
Whisky Frisky: a rhyme, *Anonymous*, 18
The Picnic Basket, *Margery Clark*, 19
Mr Puffblow's Hat, *Alf Prøysen*, 25
Mice: a poem, *Rose Fyleman*, 30
Teddy Robinson is a Red Indian, *Joan G. Robinson*, 31
Honey Bear: a poem, *Elizabeth Lang*, 43
The Three Bears, *Traditional*, 44
The Silver Thimble, *Helen Morgan*, 51
The Tree Trick, *Anita Hewett*, 58
Jacko and the Potato Scones, *Jean Sutcliffe*, 66
Johnny-Cake, *Traditional*, 72
The Marriage of the Robin and the Wren, *Norah Montgomerie*, 78
Little Trotty Wagtail: a poem, *John Clare*, 81
The Dog and the Cock, *Traditional*, 82
J for John, *Vera Colwell*, 85
Marching in our Wellingtons, *Clive Sansom*, 90
Tim Rabbit's Sneeze, *Alison Uttley*, 91
The Rain: a poem, *W. H. Davies*, 103
The Boy with the Long Name, *Anonymous*, 104
The Little Yellow Comb, *Marjorie Poppleton*, 108
The Little Woman's Water-Pot, *Lilian Daykin*, 112
The Blackbird: a poem, *Humbert Wolfe*, 120
Mr Vinegar, *Traditional*, 121
A Garage for Gabriel, *Catherine Woolley*, 127

Safety First! a participation rhyme, *Rodney Bennett*, 132
The Little Brown Egg, *Leila Berg*, 133
Charles and Jenny, *Ruth Ainsworth*, 139
The Pretty Little Hen and Bad Mr Wolf: a participation story, *Diana Ross*, 144
Blackie's Birthday, *Doris Rust*, 151
Who has seen the Wind? a poem, *Christina Rossetti*, 157
A Spring Story, *Vera Colwell*, 158
Henrietta and the Cows, *Aaron Judah*, 162
Henny-Penny, *Traditional*, 169
Just Like Me: a participation rhyme, *Anonymous*, 174
Galldora and the Rooks, *Modwena Sedgwick*, 175
Elephant Big and Elephant Little, *Anita Hewett*, 180
The Engine Driver: a participation rhyme, *Clive Sansom*, 186
Jane and the Hair Wave, *Catherine Storr*, 187
Puss and Pup, *Josef Čapek*, 192
The Old Woman and her Pig, *Traditional*, 199
Tails: a rhyme, *Anonymous*, 203
At the Seaside, *Eileen Colwell*, 204
Cuckoo! *Barbara Ker Wilson*, 210
The Magic Seeds: a poem, *James Reeves*, 217
Honk Honk! *Donald Bisset*, 218
Rat-a-Tat-Tat: a participation rhyme, *Traditional London street game*, 222
The Old Red Bus, *Jean Chapman*, 223
About Mr MacPherson's Ducks, *Marjorie Cleine*, 228
Mrs Peck Pigeon: a poem, *Eleanor Farjeon*, 235
The Jackal and the Crocodile, *Traditional*, 236
If You Find a Little Feather: a poem, *Beatrice Schenk de Regniers*, 240
All Change! *Ursula Hourihane*, 242
Good-Night: a poem, *Eleanor Farjeon*, 248
Baboushka, *Traditional*, 249
The Little Fir-Tree, *Alison Uttley*, 253
For the Storyteller, 267

The Sleepy-Mouse

ONCE upon a time, in the middle of a wood, lived a dormouse. He was more like a tiny squirrel than a mouse. He had big black eyes and fat furry ears and a thick, round, long, bushy tail.

Every summer he played in the trees, eating nuts and getting very fat. Then in the autumn, when he was plump and round, he would build a nest of moss and leaves, and put some nuts in it just for a snack. Then he would

> cover his eyes,
> and cover his nose,
> and wrap his tail right over his toes.

Then he would wrap it over his back, and over his head, and use the tip of it for a pillow. And he would go to sleep for weeks and weeks.

The dormouse never knew which he liked best. Perhaps the light warm summer when he climbed up the trees after nuts and berries;

then the sun made him so happy that sometimes, for a change, he would eat his dinner upside down, swinging from a branch by his toes. Or perhaps it was the winter he liked best, when he curled up in his soft warm nest and went to sleep; he would wake up now and then, if the weather was not too cold, and stay awake just long enough to eat a nut, then fall asleep again . . . Oh, it was a lovely life being a dormouse.

One April morning he woke up in his nest at the bottom of a hollow tree.

> He uncovered his eyes,
> he uncovered his nose,
> he unwrapped the tail that covered his toes.

He sat up and sniffed. How strange. It didn't smell like green grass and sunshine at all. It didn't smell like spring-time. He wrinkled his nose. It was a *tickly* sort of smell. He peeped out of the tree—and nearly bumped his nose on an icicle.

Everything was white. His tree was covered with inches of snow at the top, and buried in inches of snow at the bottom.

'I must have mistaken the date,' he said to himself. 'It can't be spring at all.' And he

> covered his eyes,
> and covered his nose,
> and wrapped his tail right over his toes.

And over his back, and over his head, and he used the tip of it for a pillow. But he couldn't get to sleep again.

'I'll just eat one nut,' he said to himself. 'Then I'll fall asleep easily.' He reached out his paw for a nut, but there wasn't a nut there. He'd eaten them all up.

'Tickle my whiskers,' thought the dormouse. 'I *never* eat all my nuts before spring-time.' He peeped out of the tree again, but it was just the same as before. Icicles hung like bars over his hole. And the snow was inches deep.

The dormouse sighed, for he was terribly hungry. He wasn't fat any more. He had grown thin during his long winter sleep, and he was ready to start eating again. But there was snow outside, and it couldn't be spring. So he

> covered his eyes,
> and covered his nose,
> and wrapped his tail right over his toes.

And over his back and over his head, and he used the tip of it as a pillow. But he couldn't get to sleep. He was much too hungry. And he was cold. And if there is one thing that stops anyone from going to sleep, it is being hungry and cold.

He tossed and wriggled and hunched and snuggled, but it was no use at all. He would have to get up. So he

> uncovered his eyes,
> and uncovered his nose,
> he uncurled the tail that covered his toes.

And he peeped out of the tree. Brrh. It was freezing.

Very, very carefully the dormouse climbed along the snowy twigs. The snow stuck to his paws, and he had to shake them at every step.

There was nothing green to be seen. No leaves. No grass. No spring flowers. Nothing but the thick white snow.

He ran down the twig again and on to the ground. What was a dormouse to do? His claws made patterns on the snow, as he ran this way and that, poking his nose into the thickets, hoping to find just a little snack to eat. But there was nothing, nothing at all. The dormouse was so tired with searching, that he squeezed into the hedge, and he decided

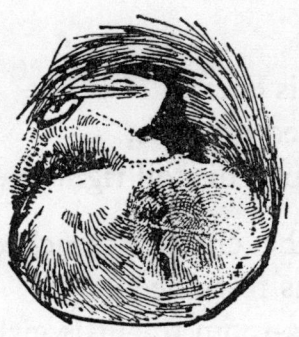

that after a little rest, he would look again.

While the dormouse was lying curled up in the hedge, some children came running along. They wore thick coats and leggings, woolly hats and wellingtons. Soon they started a snow fight, and one of the snowballs hit the hedge and made the dormouse jump. He poked his head out, wondering whatever was happening.

'Oh, a sleepy-mouse, a sleepy-mouse,' cried the children. And one little girl quickly picked up the dormouse. He was so cold and frozen, he didn't try to run away. The little girl put him inside her coat.

What a wonderful thing! All the snow that was clinging to his fur melted, and he began to feel warm again. He shook his whiskers, and curled himself up, next to her jersey.

Then he

> covered his eyes,
> and covered his nose,
> and wrapped his tail right over his toes.

And when the children reached school, the dormouse was fast asleep.

In the class-room the little girl ran up to the teacher. 'I've brought a sleepy-mouse, a sleepy-mouse,' she cried. And very, very gently she unbuttoned her coat and showed the little dormouse still fast asleep, his paws over his face.

'Was he sleeping like this when you found him? Or was he wide awake, ready for spring?' asked the teacher.

'Oh, he was awake, looking very surprised at the snow.'

'I expect he can't understand why the sun isn't shining when April's already here. He has woken up to have his first spring breakfast, and his breakfast is buried in the snow. That's what happens when we have a very bad winter. Poor little dormouse. We'll have to find something for him here instead.'

The children gathered round, while the teacher put some cotton-wool in a box, and brought a handful of corn and a saucer of water. The dormouse woke up, shook his whiskers, and settled down to breakfast. When he had finished, he lay down in the box, and

> covered his eyes,
> and covered his nose,
> and wrapped his tail right over his toes.

And he went to sleep. He stayed with the children for two weeks, until the thaw came and the snow melted. Then one day the children took him out into the field where they had found him. The sun was shining. The grass was green. And the late bluebells were opening their petals.

'Goodbye, dormouse,' they said. 'Now you can look after yourself.' And they watched him as he scampered over the grass and up the twigs of a beech tree. 'Goodbye,' they shouted. 'Goodbye, sleepy-mouse.' Then they ran back to school, for it was lesson-time again.

From *Lollipops* by Leila Berg

Whisky Frisky

Whisky Frisky,
Hipperty hop,
Up he goes
To the tree top!

Whirly, twirly,
Round and round,
Down he scampers
To the ground.

Furly, curly,
What a tail,
Tall as a feather,
Broad as a sail.

Where's his supper?
In the shell.
Snappy cracky,
Out it fell.

      Anonymous

The Picnic Basket

ONE cool summer morning Andrewshek's Auntie Katushka said, 'Andrewshek, I think I will put some sandwiches and some cottage cheese and some poppy seed cakes and two eggs in our picnic basket. Then we will go to the park and eat our lunch there, near the water.'

'May I go with you, Auntie Katushka?' said Andrewshek.

'Of course you may go to the park with me,' said Auntie Katushka. 'But first we have a great many things to do, before we can go to the park. I must go into the garden and catch the white goat. I will tie her up so she will not run away. Please find the kitten, Andrewshek, and put her in the cellar, so she will not worry the chickens while we are gone.'

'Yes, indeed, I will find the kitten and put her in the cellar,' said Andrewshek, 'so she will not worry the chickens while we are gone.'

But all Andrewshek really did was to lift

up the red and white napkin which Auntie Katushka had laid over the picnic basket and look at the eggs and the poppy seed cakes and touch the sandwiches and taste the cottage cheese.

The goat was not easy to catch. The goat wanted to go to the park, too. She galloped round and round the garden.

At last Auntie Katushka caught her and tied her firmly to the post.

Then Auntie Katushka went into the house to get Andrewshek and the lunch basket. She saw Andrewshek peeping under the red and white napkin and tasting the cottage cheese. He had forgotten all about the kitten.

The kitten was nowhere to be found. 'I think she must be paying a visit to the Mouse family,' said Auntie Katushka.

Then Auntie Katushka put on her bright shawl and took her umbrella with the long crooked handle under one arm. Then she picked up the lunch picnic basket with the red and white napkin on top and she and Andrewshek started for the park.

They went down the hill and across the railway line and past the market and down a long street until they came to the park by the water.

Andrewshek sat down on the grass beside a little stream. Andrewshek's Auntie Katushka laid her umbrella with the long crooked handle and the basket of lunch on the grass beside Andrewshek.

'Andrewshek,' said Auntie Katushka, 'I must go to the spring and get some water for us to drink. Please watch the basket with the eggs and the sandwiches and poppy seed cakes and cottage cheese while I am gone.'

'Yes, indeed, I will watch the basket of lunch,' said Andrewshek.

But what Andrewshek really did was to say to himself, 'I would like to take off my shoes and stockings and paddle in the little stream. I believe I will!'

Andrewshek took off his shoes and his stockings and went paddling in the little stream.

A big white swan came floating calmly down the stream. He saw the picnic basket lying on the grass. He stopped and stretched and stretched his long neck, till he could touch the basket. 'Honk! Honk! Honk!' said he. 'I wonder what is under the red and white napkin?'

The big white swan lifted the napkin with his red bill and looked in the basket. 'Oh, oh, oh! Won't Mother Swan be pleased with this nice lunch!' said he. 'Sandwich bread makes fine food for baby swans.'

He picked up the basket in his strong red bill and floated it ahead of him down the stream.

Andrewshek could not wade after the big swan. The water was too deep.

'Stop! Stop! White Swan!' cried Andrewshek. 'That is my Auntie Katushka's picnic basket and it has our lunch in it. Please put it back on the grass.'

'No, indeed! I will not put the basket back,' honked the big white swan. 'Sandwich bread makes fine food for baby swans and I have ten baby swans to feed.'

The big white swan gave the picnic basket a little push with his red bill. The basket floated on down the little stream. The big white swan floated calmly behind it.

Just then Andrewshek's Auntie Katushka came hurrying up with the spring water. She saw the big white swan floating down the stream, with the lunch basket floating ahead of him.

Andrewshek stood in the middle of the stream, crying.

Auntie Katushka picked up her umbrella with the long crooked handle. Auntie Katushka ran along the bank until she overtook the big white swan, with the lunch basket floating ahead of him.

She caught the handle of the picnic basket in the crook of her long-handled umbrella. She drew the basket safely to the bank.

'Well! well!' said Auntie Katushka, as she spread the red and white napkin on the grass, and laid the sandwiches and the poppy seed cakes and the cottage cheese and the eggs upon it. 'It always pays to carry an umbrella to a picnic.'

From *The Poppy Seed Cakes* by Margery Clark

Mr Puffblow's Hat

THERE was once a man called Mr Puffblow who had an enormous hat. Mr Puffblow was a very severe sort of man, and when he walked down the street he used to get very angry indeed if any of the children stared at his hat. And if they as much as stopped and looked at the house where he lived he would rush out and chase them off, because he thought they wanted to steal his apples.

Nobody dared to go against Mr Puffblow. 'Ssh!' mothers would say to their children playing in the street. 'You'd better be quiet—Mr Puffblow is coming this way!'

Every day precisely at half-past eleven Mr Puffblow walked down the street to fetch his pint of milk from the dairy. So, until *that* was over, everybody stayed indoors.

One day the West Wind came tearing through the town, and I don't think there is anything like the West Wind for upsetting things in the autumn; the mischief it gets up to is nobody's business.

Now suddenly the West Wind caught sight of Mr Puffblow walking down the street with his enormous hat on.

'Wheee!' said the West Wind. 'That's just the hat for me!'

So, with a puff and a blow, it tipped Mr Puffblow's hat off his head.

The hat bowled along the pavement. Mr Puffblow ran after it. But just as he was about to catch it, the West Wind pounced and blew it further away. This game went on for a long time until at last the West Wind carried the hat high up into the air, right over the rooftops of the town to the wood beyond.

'I'm tired of playing with you now,' said the West Wind to the hat. 'I'm going to drop you in this brook and leave you to sink or swim. Good luck!'

The hat turned two somersaults in the air, then plopped into the brook and floated away like a little round ship.

It so happened that a tiny fieldmouse had been out in the wood that day gathering nuts, and he had fallen into the brook. He could swim all right, but the current was so strong that he almost drowned struggling against it.

When he saw the hat sailing by he caught hold of the brim with his paws and clambered up to the top of the crown.

'This would make a very good ship,' thought the fieldmouse. 'I wish some of the other mice could see me now.' And he gave a loud squeak.

Sure enough, another fieldmouse heard him, and when he saw the fine-looking ship he called the other mice, and in the end there were eight little fieldmice sailing along in the hat. The one who got on first was the captain, the second was the mate and the rest were the crew.

You have no idea what fun those fieldmice had with Mr Puffblow's hat that autumn! Every day they went for a sail, and when winter came and it got too cold, they dragged the hat on to dry land and used it for a house. All through that winter they sat inside it, snug and warm, telling each other mouse fairy-tales and singing mouse-carols at Christmas.

And when spring came they started sailing again.

Then one day there was a great noise and to-do in the wood. A whole crowd of children from the town were out for a picnic. There was a man with them and they were all

laughing and shouting and having a fine time together. The man carried the smallest one on his shoulders while the others were clinging to his coat-tails. They picked flowers for him and showed him all the nicest things they could find in the wood on a spring day.

Suddenly they stopped by the brook. 'Look over there!' cried one of the children. 'Look at that big hat on the other bank!'

The mice had just dragged the hat out of the brook because they were going home to supper.

When the man saw the hat he laughed and laughed. Because, you see, he knew it.

Can you guess who he was? Mr Puffblow! But a very much nicer Mr Puffblow now, and do you know why? Well, when he used to wear that enormous hat on his head he was afraid the children would laugh at him. But from the moment he lost the hat he became quite different; he was no longer afraid.

'There's your old hat, Mr Puffblow!' shouted the children. 'Don't you want to wear it again?'

'Certainly not!' said Mr Puffblow. 'Come along now, children, let's pick flowers.'

So they did.

And the fieldmice are using Mr Puffblow's hat for a ship to this day.

From *Little Old Mrs Pepperpot* by Alf Prøysen

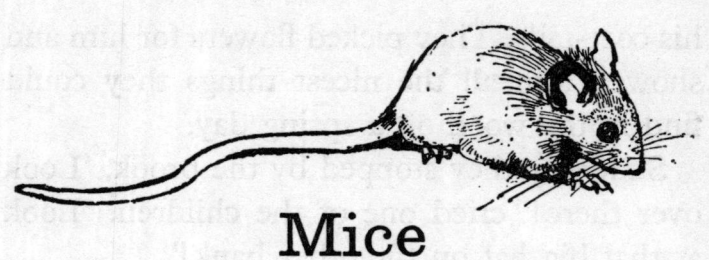

Mice

I think mice
Are rather nice.

Their tails are long,
Their faces small,
They haven't any
Chins at all.
Their ears are pink,
Their teeth are white,
They run about
The house at night.
They nibble things
They shouldn't touch
And no one seems
To like them much.

But I think mice
Are rather nice.

From *Fifty-One New Nursery Rhymes*
by Rose Fyleman

Teddy Robinson is a Red Indian

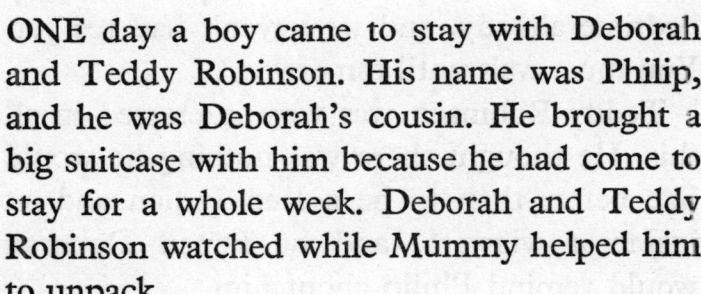

ONE day a boy came to stay with Deborah and Teddy Robinson. His name was Philip, and he was Deborah's cousin. He brought a big suitcase with him because he had come to stay for a whole week. Deborah and Teddy Robinson watched while Mummy helped him to unpack.

When they had taken out all the socks and pullovers and pyjamas and were getting near the bottom of the suitcase, they began to find some really interesting things.

First there was a Red Indian suit.

'I had it for my birthday,' said Philip.

Then two feather headdresses.

'I brought them both, in case you hadn't got one,' said Philip. 'We might want to play Red Indians.' Then there was a bow and arrow, and a little bundle of pigeons' feathers, and right at the bottom of the case, rolled up in a bundle, was a real Red Indian tent.

'That is my wigwam,' said Philip. 'It's quite big enough for both of us to get inside.'

'Oh, it's lovely!' said Deborah. 'Can we put it up in the garden?'

'Yes, of course,' said Philip. 'That's what I brought it for.'

'But not tonight,' said Mummy. 'It's nearly bedtime already, and we haven't had tea yet. You must wait until tomorrow.'

Teddy Robinson was very interested in all this. He thought there was nothing he would like better than to be a Red Indian and sit inside a wigwam, and he hoped Deborah would remind Philip about him.

But Philip was a nice boy and didn't need reminding. As soon as he saw Teddy Robinson he said, 'Hallo, you're just the kind of bear I like.' And Teddy Robinson was very pleased because Philip was just the kind of boy *he* liked. He could whistle, he could make a noise like an aeroplane with his mouth, he walked about with his hands in his pockets, and he seemed to Teddy Robinson quite the biggest and bravest boy he had ever seen.

He began to practise making aeroplane

noises himself, and wished Mummy had thought of putting pockets in his trousers. 'I should like to be as big and brave as Philip,' he said to himself.

As soon as breakfast was finished the next day, Deborah said, 'Can we put up the tent now?'

And Philip said, 'Yes. We'll be Red Indians. Let's go down into the forest and hunt wild animals.'

'Oh, yes, let's!' said Deborah. 'Where is the forest?'

'Down at the bottom of the garden,' said Philip, 'where those bushes are. We can make our camp there.'

'Oh, yes!' said Deborah. 'What fun!'

'Teddy Robinson can come too if he wants,' said Philip. 'He can guard the wigwam.'

'Hooray,' said Teddy Robinson to himself. 'That's just what I was hoping would happen.'

So Philip put on his Red Indian suit and one feather headdress, and Deborah put on a pair of pyjama trousers and the other feather headdress, and Teddy Robinson had a red doll's blanket wrapped round him and fastened with a safety pin. Then they all went down to the forest at the bottom of the garden.

'This is a good place for the wigwam,' said Philip. 'We'll put it here. Hurry and help me get it up, Debbie. I can hear some lions and tigers prowling about already.'

Teddy Robinson's fur began to feel as if it was standing up on end, but Deborah whispered to him, 'It's all right, we're only pretending,' and then his fur felt smooth again.

'Now,' said Philip. 'I'm a Red Indian brave and I've got to go and hunt those wild animals. You can be a squaw, Debbie.'

'I don't know what that is,' said Deborah, 'but I'd rather be a Red Indian too.'

'All right,' said Philip. 'We'll be two Red Indians and Teddy Robinson can be the squaw.'

'I don't think he wants to be the squaw either. Do you, Teddy Robinson?' said Deborah.

'No,' said Teddy Robinson. 'If I'm going to guard the wam-wig I'd better be a Red Indian too.'

'That's what I think,' said Deborah. 'But it's not a wam-wig, it's a wig-wam.'

'All right,' said Teddy Robinson. 'I'll call it a tent. It's easier.'

'Now, how can we make you look like a Red Indian?' said Deborah. 'The blanket's all right, but you need something on your head.'

'I know!' said Philip. 'I've got three pigeons' feathers he can have. Lend me your hair ribbon, Debbie.'

So Deborah took off her hair ribbon, and Philip tied it round Teddy Robinson's head; then he stuck the three feathers inside at the front.

'That looks fine,' said Deborah. 'You look like a real Red Indian now.'

'Good,' said Teddy Robinson. 'That's just what I feel like.'

'Now,' said Philip, 'we're going off to hunt. You sit here in the doorway, and remember that if any lions or tigers or grizzly bears come by, you're to drive them away.'

'All right,' said Teddy Robinson. 'Goodbye.'

When Philip and Deborah had gone Teddy Robinson settled down to really enjoy being a Red Indian. He sat up very straight with his tummy sticking out and practised growling and making fierce noises.

Then he began to look around to see if there were any wild animals creeping about. As he looked he saw the top leaves of the hedge moving about in the wind.

Now, that's just how a hedge would move, he thought, if a lion were walking quietly by on the other side. So he growled fiercely to frighten it away; and a moment later, when the wind stopped blowing, the top leaves of the hedge stopped moving.

'That's *one* wild animal gone,' said Teddy Robinson, and felt very brave.

Then he looked at the tool-shed which stood in a corner of the garden.

That's just the place a grizzly bear would choose to hide behind, he thought, if he happened to be in the garden and didn't want me to see him.

So he growled again and said, 'Boo-yeh-boo!' as loudly as he could.

Nothing came out from behind the tool-shed.

'Good,' said Teddy Robinson. 'That's frightened *him* away.' He was glad to think there were two wild animals less in the garden.

He began to feel rather proud of himself, and sat in the doorway of the tent waving his arms and making up a song about how brave he was.

'I'm a brave,
I'm a brave,
see how fiercely I behave!
Hear me growl
and hear me shout!
Watch me wave my arms about!
Did *any*body *ever* see
a Fiercer, Braver Bear than Me?'

Just then he heard a creeping, rustling noise in the grass behind the tent, and then the pad-pad of feet coming nearer and nearer.

Teddy Robinson knew he ought to growl and be fierce again, but he was rather out of breath with singing his brave song, and anyway he wanted to know who was coming before he drove them away. So he held his breath and decided to look tame until he knew who it was.

A moment later the next-door kitten came round the corner of the tent.

'Hello,' said the kitten in a gentle, purring voice. 'I haven't seen *you* for a long, long while.'

'Oh, it's you,' said Teddy Robinson. 'I thought you were a wild animal.'

'Did you *really*?' said the next-door kitten, rather pleased.

'Well, only for a minute,' said Teddy Robinson, 'otherwise I'd have driven you away. I'm a Red Indian, and I'm guarding the tent. I wonder, would you mind going back where you came from, and coming round the corner of the tent again? You see, I wasn't quite expecting you before, so I wasn't as fierce as I should have been.'

'Oh, yes, cer-r-r-tainly,' purred the kitten. 'I'll be a tiger,' and she scampered off very pleased.

Next time she came round the corner of the tent Teddy Robinson was ready for her, and as soon as he saw her he began to growl and shout and make very fierce noises indeed.

The next-door kitten was quite surprised. She looked at him with big round eyes and said, 'You *are* brave!'

'Yes, aren't I?' said Teddy Robinson. 'I've tamed you now, so you can come into the tent and lie down.'

'Thank you,' said the kitten, and she stepped into the tent and began to wash her paws.

Teddy Robinson looked out to see what else there was that might need taming or driving away; but there were only a few pigeons walking about on the lawn. They were pecking at the grass, and after a while they came strutting down towards the tent and began to look at Teddy Robinson, and to whisper about him.

He took no notice.

'After all, they're only pigeons,' he said to himself, 'not wild animals.'

So the pigeons came nearer and began to whisper louder.

'Coo! Look at *him*!' they said. 'He's wearing pigeons' feathers and trying to make himself look like one of us. Coo! Coo! That will never do!'

Teddy Robinson began to get cross.

'I'm *not* trying to look like a pigeon!' he shouted. 'Go away!'

'Coo! Coo!' said the pigeons. 'It's only a teddy bear dressed up.'

Teddy Robinson turned round and called softly to the next-door kitten. She had finished washing her paws, and was curled up in the tent asleep.

'Tiger!' he said. 'Do you mind waking up and coming over here?'

The kitten trotted up to him.

'Would you like to forget you are tame for a

minute,' said Teddy Robinson, 'and chase those pigeons away?'

'Oh, *yes*!' said the kitten, and pounced out of the tent. And as soon as they saw her every one of the pigeons flapped his wings and flew away.

'Well done!' said Teddy Robinson. 'You're jolly good at frightening pigeons away. I'm better at wild animals myself.'

'Yes,' said the kitten, 'we're both rather fierce really, aren't we? It's a good job we're here to guard the tent. Shall we purr a song about it?'

'Oh, yes!' said Teddy Robinson. 'But I'll growl if you don't mind. I'm not very good at purring. Shall we each make up a line in turn?'

'Yes, but I'll have the first line,' said the kitten, 'because I thought of it first.'

'All right,' said Teddy Robinson, 'and we'll both sing the last line together.' And this is the song they sang:

> 'I'm a tiger in his lair.'
> 'I'm a brave Red Indian bear.'
> 'One in fur—'
> 'And one in feather—'
> 'Here we sit on guard together.'

'I think that's rather good, don't you?' they said, nodding their heads at each other. 'Let's sing it again.'

After they had sung the song four times the kitten curled up and went to sleep, and Teddy Robinson leaned against the tent thinking how nice it was to be a fierce Red Indian having a quiet little rest.

He was nearly dropping off to sleep himself when back came Philip and Deborah.

'Hallo,' they said. 'Did you guard the tent well?'

'Yes,' said Teddy Robinson. 'I drove away a lion and a grizzly bear that were too frightened even to let me see them; and this is a tiger that I've tamed.'

'Well, you are a brave chap!' said Philip.

'I know I are,' said Teddy Robinson.

From *Teddy Robinson* by Joan G. Robinson

Honey Bear

There was a big bear
Who lived in a cave;
His greatest love
Was honey.
He had twopence a week
Which he never could save,
So he never had
Any money.
I bought him a money box
Red and round,
In which to put
His money.
He saved and saved
Till he got a pound,
Then he spent it all
On honey.

From *Book of 1000 Poems*
by Elizabeth Lang

The Three Bears

ONCE upon a time there were Three Bears, who lived together in a house of their own, in a wood. One of them was a Little, Small, Wee Bear, and one was a Middle-sized Bear, and the other was a Great, Huge Bear.

They had each a bowl for their porridge; a little bowl for the Little, Small, Wee Bear, and a middle-sized bowl for the Middle Bear, and a great bowl for the Great, Huge Bear.

And they had each a chair to sit in; a little chair for the Little, Small, Wee Bear, and a middle-sized chair for the Middle Bear, and a great chair for the Great, Huge Bear.

And they had each a bed to sleep in; a little bed for the Little, Small, Wee Bear, and a middle-sized bed for the Middle Bear, and a great bed for the Great, Huge Bear.

One day, after they had made the porridge for their breakfast, and poured it into their porridge-bowls, they walked out into the wood while the porridge was cooling, that they might not burn their mouths by beginning too soon to eat it.

And while they were walking, a little girl called Goldilocks came to the house. First she looked in at the window, and then she peeped in at the keyhole; and seeing nobody in the house, she lifted the latch. The door was not fastened, because the Bears were good Bears, who did nobody any harm, and never suspected that anybody would harm them.

So Goldilocks opened the door, and went in; and well pleased she was when she saw the porridge on the table. If she had been a good little girl, she would have waited till the Bears came home, and then, perhaps, they would have asked her to breakfast; for they were good Bears—a little rough or so, as the manner of Bears is, but for all that very good-natured and hospitable. But she set about helping herself.

So first she tasted the porridge of the Great, Huge Bear, and that was too hot for her. And then she tasted the porridge of the Middle Bear, and that was too cold for her.

And then she went to the porridge of the Little, Small, Wee Bear, and tasted that; and that was neither too hot, nor too cold, but just right; and she liked it so well, that she ate it all up.

Then Goldilocks sat down in the chair of the Great, Huge Bear, and that was too hard for her. And then she sat down in the chair of the Middle Bear, and that was too soft for her. And then she sat down in the chair of the Little, Small, Wee Bear, and that was neither too hard, nor too soft, but just right.

So she seated herself in it, and there she sat till the bottom of the chair came out, and down she came, plump upon the ground.

Then Goldilocks went upstairs into the bedchamber in which the Three Bears slept. And first she lay down upon the bed of the Great, Huge Bear; but that was too high at the head for her. And next she lay down upon the bed of the Middle Bear; and that was too high at the foot for her. And then she lay down upon the bed of the Little, Small, Wee Bear; and that was neither too high at the head, nor too high at the foot, but just right. So she covered herself up comfortably, and lay there till she fell fast asleep.

By this time the Three Bears thought their porridge would be cool enough; so they came home to breakfast. Now Goldilocks had left the spoon of the Great, Huge Bear standing in his porridge.

'SOMEBODY HAS BEEN AT MY PORRIDGE!' said the Great, Huge Bear, in his great, rough, gruff voice.

And when the Middle Bear looked at hers, she saw that the spoon was standing in it too.

'SOMEBODY HAS BEEN AT MY PORRIDGE!' said the Middle Bear, in her middle voice.

Then the Little, Small, Wee Bear looked at his, and there was the spoon in the porridge bowl, but the porridge was all gone.

'SOMEBODY HAS BEEN AT MY PORRIDGE, AND HAS EATEN IT ALL UP!' said the Little, Small, Wee Bear, in his little, small, wee voice.

Upon this the Three Bears, seeing that someone had entered their house, and eaten up the Little, Small, Wee Bear's breakfast, began to look about them. Now Goldilocks had not put the hard cushion straight when she rose from the chair of the Great, Huge Bear.

'SOMEBODY HAS BEEN SITTING IN MY CHAIR!' said the Great, Huge Bear in his great, rough, gruff voice.

And Goldilocks had pressed down the soft cushion of the Middle Bear.

'SOMEBODY HAS BEEN SITTING IN MY CHAIR!' said the Middle Bear, in her middle voice.

And you know what Goldilocks had done to the third chair.

'SOMEBODY HAS BEEN SITTING IN MY CHAIR AND HAS SAT THE BOTTOM OUT OF IT!' said the Little, Small, Wee Bear in his little, small, wee voice.

Then the Three Bears thought it necessary

that they should make further search; so they went upstairs into their bedchamber. Now Goldilocks had pulled the pillow of the Great, Huge Bear out of its place.

'SOMEBODY HAS BEEN LYING IN MY BED!' said the Great, Huge Bear in his great, rough, gruff voice.

And Goldilocks had pulled the bolster of the Middle Bear out of its place.

'SOMEBODY HAS BEEN LYING IN MY BED!' said the Middle Bear in her middle voice.

And when the Little, Small, Wee Bear came to look at his bed, there was the bolster in its place; and the pillow in its place upon the bolster; and upon the pillow was Goldilocks' head—which was not in its place, for she had no business there.

'SOMEBODY HAS BEEN LYING IN MY BED—AND HERE SHE IS!' said the Little, Small, Wee Bear, in his little, small, wee voice.

Little Goldilocks had heard in her sleep the great, rough, gruff voice of the Great, Huge Bear, but she was so fast asleep that it was no more to her than the roaring of wind or the rumbling of thunder.

And she had heard the middle voice of the Middle Bear, but it was only as if she had heard someone speaking in a dream.

But when she heard the little, small, wee voice of the Little, Small, Wee Bear, it was so sharp, and so shrill, that it awakened her at once. Up she started; and when she saw the Three Bears on one side of the bed, she tumbled herself out at the other and ran to the window. Now the window was open, because the Bears, like good, tidy Bears, as they were, always opened their bedchamber window when they got up in the morning. Out jumped Goldilocks and ran off into the wood.

What happened to her no one knows, but the Three Bears never set eyes on her again.

Traditional

The Silver Thimble

MARY KATE woke up one morning with the feeling that something rather special was going to happen. She lay quite still for a few minutes, trying to think what it could be. Then she remembered. Today was Saturday and Auntie Dot and Uncle Ned were coming for the weekend.

Mary Kate leaned over the side of her bed and lifted her best doll, Dorabella, out of the dolls' cot, and began to dress her. She was just buttoning Dorabella's pinafore when she heard the alarm clock ringing and a moment or two later Mummy went downstairs.

Tucking Dorabella under her arm, Mary Kate climbed out of bed and followed Mummy down.

'Good gracious me!' cried Mummy, when she saw Mary Kate. 'There was no need for you to get up early as well. And Dorabella dressed already!'

'I put her best clothes on,' explained Mary Kate, 'because of Auntie Dot and Uncle Ned. She's wearing her pinafore to keep her frock clean. She can sit quietly on my little chair until it's time to go out.'

'Is she going out then?' asked Mummy in surprise.

'Oh, yes,' said Mary Kate. 'I told her last night she could go to the station with us to meet the train.'

'Well, I'm afraid I shan't have time to go,' Mummy said. 'I have far too much to do in the house, and I want to make one of Uncle Ned's favourite fruit and nut cakes. Daddy will have to take you.'

'All right,' said Mary Kate. 'May I have my breakfast now, please?'

'Go and put your dressing-gown on first,' Mummy said, 'and tell Daddy breakfast will be ready in ten minutes.'

After breakfast Mary Kate and Daddy went upstairs to get dressed. Mummy cleared the table and washed up and then she began to make the fruit cake.

When Mary Kate was ready except for her hat and coat she sat on a chair and waited for Daddy to finish dressing. He was just fastening his shirt when one of the buttons jumped off and rolled across the floor.

'Oh dear,' said Daddy. 'Where did that go?'

'Under the bed, I think,' Mary Kate told him—and she knelt down to look. 'I can see it,' she grunted, peering under the bed, 'but I can't reach it.'

So Daddy had to go down on the floor beside her and stretch out his long arm for the button.

'Hold it for me, Mary Kate,' he said, 'while I fasten my shoelaces. I shall have to go and ask Mummy to sew it on again.'

When the shoelaces were fastened Daddy went downstairs to Mummy's workbox, took out a needle and threaded it with white cotton. Then he took the needle into the kitchen. Mary Kate followed him, carrying the button.

Mummy wiped her floury hands on her apron.

'I must have my thimble,' she said. 'I can't sew without it. Run and fetch it for me, will you, Mary Kate?'

Mary Kate ran to Mummy's workbox and took out the silver thimble. She put it in her pocket to keep it safe, closed the workbox and went back to the kitchen.

Daddy stood quite still while Mummy sewed the button on his shirt and then he took the needle and cotton and put them away again. Mummy went on making the fruit cake, and Mary Kate put on her hat and coat and waited for Daddy in the hall.

Mummy was putting the cake mixture into the baking tin when Daddy came downstairs again. 'We're off now,' he called, fastening Mary Kate's coat properly and straightening her hat for her. 'We shan't be long.'

'All right,' called Mummy. 'Goodbye.'

'Goodbye,' shouted Mary Kate and, 'Goodbye,' said Daddy, and they set off down the hill towards the station.

They hadn't gone very far when Mary Kate suddenly remembered Dorabella.

'I forgot all about her because of the button,' she said. 'She's sitting in my little chair waiting to be taken out.'

'Oh dear,' said Daddy, looking at his watch. 'We haven't a great deal of time now. Surely she won't mind being left behind just this once, will she?'

'Yes, she will,' said Mary Kate. 'I promised her she could come with us. She'll cry if we don't take her.'

'Oh well,' sighed Daddy, 'if you promised, that's different. You wait here and I'll run back for her.'

Off he went back up the hill, while Mary Kate waited on the narrow footpath. In a minute or two Daddy came running back with Dorabella under his arm.

'You were quite right,' he said, giving her to Mary Kate. 'She looked as though she was going to cry.'

'She's still got her pinafore on,' said Mary Kate.

'Well, you'll have to take it off when we get to the station,' Daddy told her. 'We must hurry now, or Auntie Dot and Uncle Ned will be there before us.' They hurried down the hill and arrived at the station just as the train came in. Auntie Dot was looking out of the carriage window and she waved to Mary Kate, who couldn't wave back because she was trying to unfasten Dorabella's pinafore.

Daddy went to find a taxi while Uncle Ned collected the luggage. 'I'm on holiday,' he said, 'and carrying a case uphill is too much like hard work for my liking.'

Mary Kate was very pleased. Dorabella had never been in a taxi before.

Mummy had coffee and biscuits ready for them when they got home and the fruit cake in the oven was beginning to smell spicy and nice.

'I've dropped my silver thimble somewhere,' said Mummy as she poured some milk into Mary Kate's mug. 'Will you see if you can find it for me, pet?'

Mary Kate put Dorabella into her pram and began to look for the thimble. She searched and searched but she couldn't see it anywhere. She had just stopped for a minute to drink her milk when Uncle Ned came into the kitchen.

'Mummy says you're playing "Hunt the Thimble",' he said, 'so I've come to join you.'

He moved the little cupboard and looked under the doormat and poked behind the cooker with the broom handle. Mary Kate peered into the peg bag and peeped into the vegetable rack and the dog basket, but they couldn't find the thimble anywhere.

'Never mind,' said Mummy, coming in with the coffee tray and putting it on the table. 'I expect I shall find it when I sweep.'

She moved Mary Kate out of the way and opened the oven door to peep at the cake.

'That smells jolly good,' said Uncle Ned.

It *was* good. They had it for tea. Uncle Ned had one big slice and then he had another and then he said he thought he could manage a third.

He pulled the plate towards him and began to cut a slice. Half-way through the knife stuck.

'Hallo,' said Uncle Ned. 'What's this?' He poked in the cake with the point of the knife and something tinkled down on to the plate.

It was Mummy's silver thimble!

'Well,' said Uncle Ned, eating up all the crumbs he had made. 'I've had cherry cake and coffee cake and seed cake, but this is the first time I've ever had Thimble Cake! Jolly good it is, too!'

From *Meet Mary Kate* by Helen Morgan

The Tree Trick

A MORA tree and a mango tree grew side by side in the jungle. High between the topmost branches a thick creeper rope stretched from tree to tree like a clothes line.

In the mora tree lived the monkey family—Father Monkey, Mother Monkey, and three little smiling monkey children.

Mother and Father sat on the ground, eating juicy mora berries. The three smiling children climbed in the tree, happily playing a circus game. They went to the end of the topmost branch and hung by their hands from the creeper rope. They moved their hands along the rope, swinging across to the mango tree. Then they hid in its branches and no one could see them.

'What are they up to *now*?' said their father. 'They're very quiet all of a sudden.'

'It's only the circus game,' said their mother.

She looked up into the mora tree. No one

was there. 'They have gone,' she said. 'They have gone across the creeper rope and they're hiding themselves in the mango tree.'

Father Monkey called: 'Come down. There are juicy mora berries for supper. Come down here, you little monkeys.'

The monkey children came from the mango tree, swinging across the creeper rope to the topmost branch of their own home tree. Then they jumped down the tree from branch to branch and sat in a row to eat their supper.

Along the track bounded great cat Panther, fierce and hungry and hunting for supper. With a thud and a growl he stopped by the tree.

'Ah! My supper at last,' he said. 'Five little fat delicious monkeys!'

The monkey children shook with fright.

'But our skins are tough,' said Father Monkey. 'We're hairy and bony and not nice-tasting. Wouldn't you rather eat a goat, or a sheep, or a nice little tender weasel?'

'No,' said Panther. 'I want to eat *you*.'

Father Monkey looked at his children.

'It's really rather strange,' he said. 'The rules must be different for panthers and monkeys.'

'What rules?' Panther wanted to know.

'The eating rules,' said Father Monkey. 'In the monkey tribe the rule is this: Children eat first, grown-ups after.'

Panther looked at the monkey children.

'Have they eaten their supper yet?' he asked.

Father Monkey said: 'Oh no, they were just going to start when *you* came along.'

'I suppose we must keep to the rules,' said Panther. 'Children eat first, grown-ups after. *They* are children and I'm a grown-up. They must have their supper before I have mine. Tell them to go and get it, Monkey. But tell them to hurry, and come back quickly.'

Father Monkey looked at the children.

'Go and get your supper,' he said. 'It's up on the topmost branch of the mora tree. Eat it quickly, as Panther tells you.'

He shook his paw at the three little monkeys.

'Don't waste time, do you hear, little monkeys. Don't start playing the circus game.'

But as he spoke, he winked an eye.

The little monkeys said, 'Yes, Father, we know *exactly* what you mean.' And up they climbed, until no one could see them.

Panther sat on the ground, waiting.

But the monkey children did not come back.

Panther began to yawn and fidget.

'Why are they taking so long?' he asked.

Father Monkey scratched his head.

'I expect it's because of the rules,' he said.

'What rules?' Panther wanted to know.

'The starting rules,' said Father Monkey. 'In the monkey tribe the rule is this: Children do not eat their supper till Mother Monkey tells them to start.'

'I suppose we must keep to the rules,' said Panther. 'Your children can't start, so how can they finish? Until they have finished, they can't come back. If they don't come back, where is my supper? Tell your wife to climb the tree, so that her monkey children may start.'

Father Monkey smiled and said: 'Monkey wife, go up the tree. Tell the children to eat their supper. Then bring them back quickly, for Panther is hungry.'

But as he spoke he winked an eye.

Mother Monkey said: 'My dear, I understand *perfectly* what you mean.' She climbed and climbed until no one could see her.

Panther sat on the ground, waiting.

But Mother Monkey did not come back. Nor did the little monkey children.

Panther began to sigh and shuffle.

'Why is she taking so long?' he asked.

Father Monkey waved a paw.

'I expect it's because of the rules,' he said.

'What rules?' Panther wanted to know.

'The coming down rules,' said Father Monkey. 'In the monkey tribe the rule is this: Mother follows Father's tail.'

Panther growled in his throat and said, 'I am growing tired of these rules, rules, rules. Climb up the tree, and then come back, and tell your wife to follow your tail. And don't forget to bring the children.'

'Just as you say,' said Father Monkey. And away he went, climbing fast.

Panther waited, yawning and fidgeting.

He waited still longer, sighing and shuffling.

'Why are you taking so long?' he shouted. 'Come down here, or I'll climb up and fetch you.'

There was no answer.

Panther started to climb through the

branches, but he could not see the five fat monkeys. He *did* see the creeper rope stretching out, joined to the mango tree like a clothes line.

'I mustn't step on *that*,' he said. 'It's much too thin for a panther's weight.'

He stood at last on the topmost branch, but not a tail or a paw could he see. And then he was quite the most puzzled panther that ever lost a monkey family.

'Where can they be?' he said to himself. 'They are certainly not in this mora tree. And they didn't come down, so they must have gone up.'

He stared up into the empty sky.

'How did they do it?' he said to himself. 'How did they climb up and up to the top, and suddenly vanish to nothing at all?'

Panther climbed down, sadly and slowly, because he was trying to think of an answer. He went far away, without any supper, and thought all that evening, and all the next day, and the day after that. But his thinking was useless. None of his answers was right, and he knew it.

The only right answer was back in the jungle, where the mora and mango trees grew, side by side. From the topmost branch of the mango tree came Father Monkey, Mother Monkey, and three little smiling monkey children. They went one by one to the end of the branch, and hung from the creeper rope by their hands. They moved their hands along the rope, swinging across to the mora tree.

'It's good to be back again,' they said. 'It's good to be back in our own home tree.'

Then they smiled at each other, and ate their supper.

> From *A Hat for Rhinoceros* by Anita Hewett

Jacko and the Potato Scones

NOW most of the time Jacko was a good little monkey. But sometimes he was naughty, and even when Mrs Robb said, 'No, *no*, Jacko, you must not do that,' he would go on and do that very thing.

Well, one day Mrs Robb was busy, because four people were coming to tea. That meant she had to do a lot of cooking. So she shut Jacko in his cage, and said, 'You must stay there till I've finished, Jacko, or you'll be in the way.'

And Jacko understood and smiled and chattered as if to say, 'That's all right.'

He sat quietly in his cage and watched Mrs Robb and even went into the dark part of his cage, and lay down on the soft old shawl that was there, and had a short rest. When he came out again he was feeling very lively. He saw that Mrs Robb had put a plate of thin potato scones close to the fire. They were lovely potato scones—thin and whitish with brown spots on them, and almost as big as a dinner plate. They were piled one on top of the other. When tea-time came Mrs Robb would spread each one with butter and jam, and roll them up and they'd be lovely to eat—all squashy and soft and buttery and sweet.

Jacko was feeling a bit cold. He wished he could go and sit on his little stool near the fire and be as warm as the thin potato scones. So he chattered a bit, for he thought he'd like someone to know about this, and he shivered a bit and rubbed his little hands together.

Just then Mr Robb came into the kitchen, so Jacko told him all about what he was wanting to do.

'Hello, Jacko,' said Mr Robb. 'Want to come out?'

Jacko chattered yes he did—and would Mr Robb do something about it please.

Mr Robb opened the door of the cage. Jacko dropped down on to the floor, ran across to the fire, and whoops! he landed light as a leaf on his little stool. He held out his hands to the fire and turned his head to smile happily at Mr Robb.

'Cold were you?' said Mr Robb.

And Jacko chattered that he was—very cold—but he'd soon be warm now.

Presently Mr Robb went out of the kitchen and Jacko sat alone looking at the plate of big, thin, warm potato scones.

Then he stretched out his hand and picked one up. It was like a little mat, so he put it on his stool and sat on it. It felt nice and warm. Then he picked another up and put it on his head. He had a very little head, you know, so it hung down all round—he couldn't see. Jacko didn't like that, so he made two holes to look through in the part that came over his face.

Jacko was rather pleased with himself, and sat there on his potato scone mat feeling that he'd been very clever. Then his back felt a bit cold. He couldn't move about much or the scone would fall off his head, so he put his hand out, and took another one off the plate, and put it round his shoulders like a shawl. Ah! That felt nice and warm! And there he sat, and almost went to sleep he was so warm and comfortable.

Well, suddenly the door opened, and in came Mrs Robb. 'I must let Jacko out of his cage now,' she said to herself, and she went to

the cage to do this. The door was open, and the cage was empty.

'Now how did he get out?' said Mrs Robb. 'And where is he?'

Then she turned round and saw something very queer sitting up on the little stool in front of the fire.

'Oh,' she cried. 'What's that? Jacko! Is that you?'

Jacko turned his head and looked at Mrs Robb through the two holes in the scone that was over his face.

'Jacko!' said Mrs Robb. 'What will you do next?' And he looked so funny that she began to laugh, and she laughed so much that she had to sit down. And Mr Robb heard her and came into the kitchen and said, 'What's the matter?'

'Look,' said Mrs Robb, and she pointed at Jacko.

Then Mr Robb started to laugh, and he laughed so much that he had to sit down. And they both laughed and laughed till they had no breath left.

But Jacko didn't like them laughing. *He* thought he was a *clever* little monkey, not a funny one.

He took the potato scone off his head and put it carefully back on the plate; he took the one off his shoulders and put it on top of the other one. Then he put the one he'd been sitting on on top of that.

Then he got off his stool and walked across the floor, and jumped up into his cage and went into the little dark bedroom part, and covered himself up with the soft old shawl and he didn't come out till after tea, although the door was left wide open.

Wasn't he a funny little monkey?

From *Jacko and Other Stories* by Jean Sutcliffe

Johnny-Cake

ONCE upon a time there was an old man, and an old woman, and a little boy. One morning the old woman made a Johnny-cake, and put it in the oven to bake. 'You watch the Johnny-cake while your father and I go out to work in the garden.'

So the old man and the old woman went out and began to hoe potatoes, and left the little boy to tend the oven. But he didn't watch it all the time, and all of a sudden he heard a noise, and he looked up and the oven door popped open, and out of the oven jumped Johnny-cake, and went rolling along end over end, towards the open door of the house. The little boy ran to shut the door, but Johnny-cake was too quick for him, and rolled through the door, down the steps, and out into the road long before the little boy could catch him. The little boy ran after him as fast as he could clip it, crying out to his father and mother, who heard the uproar, and threw down their hoes

and gave chase too. But Johnny-cake outran all three a long way, and was soon out of sight, while they had to sit down, all out of breath, on a bank to rest.

On went Johnny-cake, and by-and-by he came to two well-diggers who looked up from their work and called out: 'Where are ye going, Johnny-cake?'

He said: 'I've outrun an old man, and an old woman, and a little boy, and I can outrun you too—o—o!'

'Ye can, can ye? We'll see about that!' said they, and they threw down their picks and ran after him, but couldn't catch up with him, and soon they had to sit down by the roadside to rest.

On ran Johnny-cake, and by-and-by he came to two ditch-diggers who were digging a ditch. 'Where are ye going, Johnny-cake?' said they. He said: 'I've outrun an old man, and an old woman, and a little boy, and two well-diggers, and I can outrun you too—o—o!'

'Ye can, can ye? We'll see about that!' said they; and they threw down their spades, and ran after him too. But Johnny-cake soon outstripped them also, and seeing they could never catch him, they gave up the chase and sat down to rest.

On went Johnny-cake, and by-and-by he came to a bear. The bear said: 'Where are ye going, Johnny-cake?'

He said: 'I've outrun an old man, and an old woman, and a little boy, and two well-diggers, and two ditch-diggers, and I can outrun you too—o—o!'

'Ye can, can ye?' growled the bear. 'We'll see about that!' and trotted as fast as his legs could carry him after Johnny-cake, who never stopped to look behind him. Before long the bear was left so far behind that he saw he might as well give up the hunt first as last, so he stretched himself out by the roadside to rest.

On went Johnny-cake, and by-and-by he came to a wolf. The wolf said: 'Where are ye going, Johnny-cake?'

He said: 'I've outrun an old man, and an old woman, and a little boy, and two well-diggers, and two ditch-diggers and a bear, and I can outrun you too—o—o!'

'Ye can, can ye?' snarled the wolf, 'We'll see about that!' And he set off into a gallop after Johnny-cake, who went on and on so fast that the wolf too saw there was no hope of overtaking him, and he too lay down to rest.

On went Johnny-cake, and by-and-by he came to a fox that lay quietly in a corner of the fence. The fox called out in a sharp voice, but without getting up: 'Where are ye going, Johnny-cake?'

He said: 'I've outrun an old man, and an old woman, and a little boy, and two well-diggers and two ditch-diggers, a bear and a wolf, and I can outrun you too—o—o!'

The fox said: 'I can't quite hear you, Johnny-cake, won't you come a little closer?' turning his head a little to one side.

Johnny-cake stopped his race for the first time, and went a little closer, and called out in a very loud voice: *'I've outrun an old man, and an old woman, and a little boy, and two well-diggers, and two ditch-diggers, and a bear, and a wolf, and I can out run you too—o—o!'*

'Can't quite hear you; won't you come a *little* closer?' said the fox in a feeble voice, as he stretched out his neck towards Johnny-cake, and put one paw behind his ear.

Johnny-cake came up close, and, leaning towards the fox screamed out: 'I'VE OUTRUN AN OLD MAN, AND AN OLD WOMAN, AND A LITTLE BOY, AND TWO WELL-DIGGERS AND TWO

DITCH-DIGGERS, AND A BEAR, AND A WOLF, AND I CAN OUTRUN YOU TOO—O—O!'

'You can, can you?' yelped the fox, and he snapped up the Johnny-cake in his sharp teeth in the twinkling of an eye.

Traditional

The Marriage of the Robin and the Wren

THERE was once an old Grey Cat who went down by the river bank. There she saw a wee Robin Redbreast hopping on a briar.

'Where are you going, wee Robin?' said she.

'I'm away to sing the King a song this good Yule morning,' said wee Robin.

'Come here, wee Robin, and see the bonny white ring round my neck.'

But wee Robin said: 'No, no, Grey Cat, no, no. You caught the wee Mouse but you'll not catch me.' And off he flew to the dry stone dyke. There he saw a greedy Hawk who said: 'Where are you going, wee Robin?'

'I'm away to sing the King a song this good Yule morning,' said the wee Robin.

'Come here and see the bonny feathers in my wing.'

'No, no, greedy Hawk, no, no. You pecked the wee Linnet but you'll not peck me.' And

off he flew to some steep rocks where the sly Fox was sitting.

'Where are you going, wee Robin,?' said he.

'I'm away to sing the King a song this good Yule morning.'

'Come here, wee Robin, and I'll show you the bonny spot on the tip of my tail.'

But wee Robin said: 'No, no, sly Fox, no,

no. You worried the wee Lamb, but you'll not worry me.' And off he flew until he came to the side of a brook. There he saw a young lad who said: 'Where are you going, wee Robin?'

'I'm away to sing the King a song this good Yule morning.'

'Come here, wee Robin, and I'll show you my grand collection of marbles from my pocket.'

But wee Robin said: 'No, no, Laddie, no, no. You captured the Chaffinch but you'll not capture me.' And off he flew until he came at last to the King's palace, and there he sat on a window sill and sang the King a bonny song. The King was very pleased and he said to the Queen: 'What shall we give wee Robin for singing us such a bonny song?'

And the Queen said: 'Let us give him the wee Wren to be his wife.'

And so Robin Redbreast and the wee Wren were married, and the King and the Queen and the whole court danced at their wedding.

From *Twenty-five Fables* by Norah Montgomerie

Little Trotty Wagtail

Little trotty wagtail, he went in the rain,
And tittering tottering sideways, he near got straight again.
He stooped to get a worm, and look'd up to catch a fly,
And then he flew away ere his feathers they were dry.
Little trotty wagtail, he waddled in the mud,
And left his little footmarks, trample where he would.
He waddled in the water-pudge, and waggle went his tail,
And chirrupt up his wings to dry upon the garden rail.
Little trotty wagtail, you nimble all about,
And in the dimpling water-pudge you waddle in and out;
Your home is nigh at hand, and in the warm pigsty,
So, little Master Wagtail, I'll bid you a good-bye.

John Clare

The Dog and the Cock

ONCE upon a time a man who had a dog and a cock had no food to give them, because his crops had failed. So the dog said to the cock: 'Well, brother Peter, I think we should get more food to eat if we went and lived in the forest than here at our master's, don't you?' 'Yes,' said the cock, 'let's be off, there's no help for it.'

So they said goodbye to their master and mistress and went off to see what they could find. And they went on and on, but couldn't find a nice place to stop in. Then it began to grow dark, and the cock said: 'Let's spend the night on a tree. I'll fly up on to a branch, and you get into the hole under the tree. We'll pass the night somehow.'

So the cock made his way to a branch, tucked in his toes, and went to sleep, and the dog made himself a bed under the tree. And they slept all night; and in the morning, when it began to get light, the cock woke up and crowed as loudly as he could: 'Cock-a-doodle-do! Cock-a-doodle-doo! All wake up! All get up! The sun will soon be rising, and the day will soon begin!'

And he crowed so loudly, that a fox nearby heard him and said to himself: 'What a funny thing for a cock to be crowing in the forest! He must have lost his way and can't get out again!'

And he began to look for the cock, and after a bit he saw him sitting upon the branch of the tree. 'Oho!' said the fox to himself, 'he'd make a fine meal! How can I get him to come down from there?'

So he went up to the tree and said to the cock: 'What a fine cock you are! I've never seen such a fine one in all my days! What lovely feathers, just as if they were covered with gold! And your tail! I can't tell you how fine it is! And what a sweet voice you've got! I could listen to it all day and all night. Do come a little nearer and let's get to know each other a little better. I've got a party on at my place today, and I shall have lots of food and drink for you if you will come. Let's go along to my home.'

'Very well,' said the cock, 'I'll come, only you must ask my friend too. We always go

about together.' 'And where is your friend?' asked the fox. 'Down below in the hole under the tree,' said the cock. And the fox poked his head into the hole, thinking there was another cock there, when the dog popped his head out and caught Mr Fox by the nose!

Traditional story from *Picture Tales from the Russian*, illustrated by Valery Carrick

J for John

JOHN was very excited for it was his birthday—and what luck, it was snowing!

He ran downstairs to breakfast in great excitement. The table was laid for breakfast and there was a special brown egg for him. But instead of the usual pile of presents beside his plate, there was only one little box.

John felt very disappointed. Was he only going to have one present this year?

His mother smiled. 'Open that box, dear, and see what's inside it,' she said.

John opened it. Inside there were three keys—a big one, a middle-sized one and a small one. There was a piece of paper too, and on it was printed a big letter 'J'.

'What is it, Mummy?' he asked. He felt very puzzled.

'Well,' said his mother, 'your father and I thought that as it's not long since you had your Christmas presents, you might like to have your birthday presents in a different kind of way. We've hidden three presents for you. When you find out where these keys fit, you'll find your presents too. Each one will have a big "J for John" tied on to it so that you will know it is yours.'

'Can I begin looking now?' asked John eagerly.

'When you've eaten your breakfast.'

Breakfast over, John had a good look at the three keys. 'I'll try the middle one first,' he decided. 'It looks the easiest.' He ran round the house in a great hurry, trying to fit the key in all kinds of locks. Some were too large so that the key almost disappeared in them, others were too small so that the key wouldn't go in at all. He had no luck downstairs, so went upstairs to his mother's room. He tried the drawer in the dressing-table and the chest of drawers and, last of all, the wardrobe. The key fitted—CLICK—it turned and he looked inside.

There were his mother's dresses and her fur coat. John rubbed his face against it—he liked its softness. But where was his present? He rummaged about and there was a box. Tied to it was a label with a big 'J for John' on it.

He sat down on the floor to open the box. Inside was a pair of wellingtons, real boy's wellingtons. 'I'll be able to go out in the snow even when it's as deep as deep,' he thought.

Now he chose the small key. It was too small for the doors of the rooms, too big for his mother's little bureau. But one of the drawers in the sideboard was locked and when he fitted the key in the keyhole, CLICK, it turned. Inside among the tablecloths was a parcel wrapped in gay paper and tied on to it was a label with a big 'J' printed on it.

John tore open the paper. There was a special kind of woollen cap with flaps to go over his ears—just like the one his father had brought back from Canada. Now his ears would be warm in the snow.

There was only the big key left. 'Wherever does this one fit?' he asked his mother.

'I mustn't tell you,' she said, 'but I *think* you've often seen someone using it.'

John sat down by the fire and thought. Whoever would use a big key like that? Why, his father of course! 'I know,' he shouted, 'it's the key to the shed. Can I go outside in the snow and try it?'

'Wrap up warmly,' said his mother.

'I shall put on my new wellingtons,' said John busily, 'and my new cap.'

'And your coat,' said his mother.

Soon John was dressed and ready. He opened the door. Brrrr—how cold it was. The lawn was white and smooth except for the little criss-cross marks made by the birds' feet. He put his foot in the snow—it was quite deep. But his father had cleared a path to the garage and to the shed.

Big flakes of snow were falling and tickling his nose. He plodded to the shed door and put the big key in the lock. It fitted. He had to use both hands to turn it, but—CLICK—it opened the door.

Inside the shed were his father's garden tools and his lawn mower. There was the wheelbarrow, and where was his present? Suddenly he saw it—a large parcel wrapped in brown paper and on top of it was a label, 'J for John'.

Whatever could be inside the parcel? It was quite long but not very tall. He tore a corner of the paper and peeped through. He could see something red and made of wood. Could it be—? He stripped off the paper in a hurry—yes, it was a sledge, the thing he had wanted

more than anything! It was a beauty too—painted bright blue and red with shining runners and a thick white cord to pull it by.

What a good thing it was Saturday tomorrow and his father would have a holiday. What fun they would have!

And so they did, rushing down the hill on the sledge, falling into the snow and climbing the hill to do it all over again.

It was the most exciting birthday John had ever had.

Vera Colwell

Marching in our Wellingtons

Marching in our wellingtons,
 Tramp, tramp, tramp,
Marching in our wellingtons,
 We won't get damp.

Splashing through the puddles
 In the rain, rain, rain—
Splashing through the puddles,
 And splashing home again!

From *Speech Rhymes* edited by Clive Sansom

Tim Rabbit's Sneeze

ONE day it rained and rained without stopping. The streams were swollen to little rivers, and new streams came running down the lanes, tearing up the stones, and sweeping the leaves before them. Pools formed in the hollows, and ponds filled every hole and dimple on the common. Little Tim Rabbit stood at the door of the small cottage watching the bouncing rain.

'Can I go out, Mother?' he asked.

'No, Tim,' said Mrs Rabbit, shaking her head. 'No. You would get wet to the skin.'

'I wish I had a mushroom umbrella,' sighed Tim.

Five minutes later he asked again.

'Can I go fishing, Mother?'

'Certainly not,' said Mrs Rabbit. 'Even the fish have gone into their houses to play.'

'I wish I were a fish,' sighed Tim.

He took a piece of chalk and made some

squares on the kitchen floor. Then he played hopscotch, dancing and hopping in and out of the squares, with a stone balanced on his fur toe.

Next he played marbles, and rolled his little clay marbles in the hollows of the floor.

He helped his mother to bake a cake, and he sat on the hearth and sang a song.

At last the rain stopped and the sun began to shine with a watery face. Tim looked out at the wet world. 'Can I go out now, Mother?' he asked.

'Yes, Tim, but keep away from the rain pools,' said Mrs Rabbit.

Tim fetched his fishing-rod from the corner and ran outside. Every little pool and streamlet reflected the sunbeams. The common was all a-glitter. Rain-drops shone like gold, and sparkled like fish-scales.

'There must be lots of goldfish there,' thought Tim.

He went across the wet grass, and sat by the edge of a small newly-made pond. It was rippled with little waves, and each wave was tipped with sunlight. At the bottom of the water Tim could see the daisies and buttercups growing. He dipped his hazel rod into the pond and waited for a fish to bite.

> 'Little Tom Fishy,
> Come to my dishy,
> Come to be fried in our frying-pan,'

he called, and the waves flashed and the water laughed at little Tim.

From the boughs of an overhanging tree a bird looked down. It spread its feathers to dry them in the sun, and lifted a leg, and winked at Tim.

'Tim Rabbit! Tim Rabbit!' it called. 'You'll never catch a fish that way.'

'Hello, Magpie,' said Tim, looking into the leafy branches at the bright eye and the gleaming feathers of the wicked bird.

'The goldfish won't nibble at your bait, Tim. They like something special,' said the Magpie.

'What do they like?' asked Tim.

'Throw away your fishing-rod and dangle your feet in the water. They will nibble your toes,' said the Magpie.

'I shouldn't like that,' said Tim, quickly.

'They have no teeth, Tim. They'll only tickle you. When you feel a sweet tickle, grab the little goldfish from the water.'

'Thank you, Magpie. I never knew that,' said Tim humbly, and he dangled his little furry toes in the water. For a long time he sat, and the sun went in, and the gold waves became dark. A cloud passed over the sky, Tim's toes were very cold and he shivered, and then he sneezed.

'What are you doing there, sitting in the water, Tim Rabbit?' scolded the Hedgehog.

'Fishing for goldfish,' said Tim.

'There ain't no fish, goldfish or silverfish, in that rain-water pool. Get you home at once, Tim Rabbit, and warm yourself by the fire, or you'll catch a cold.'

Tim climbed out of the water, and he sneezed again. He felt very wet and rather miserable. He ran unsteadily, for his legs were stiff.

'Mercy me, Tim!' cried Mrs Rabbit. 'Where have you been? Your feet are soaking wet, and your nose is blue and your eyes are watering.' She held up her paws in horror. She seized her little son and dried him with a warm towel and rubbed him with hay. Then she put him on a stool by the fire.

'A-tishoo! A-tishoo!' sneezed Tim.

'Deary me!' cried Mrs Rabbit. 'You'll sneeze

the roof off. The house isn't as strong as it was. The roof was never mended after that gale in March.'

Tim sneezed again, and the roof of the little house shook.

'I must send the sneeze away or the house will fall down,' cried Mrs Rabbit in alarm.

She made Tim some hot blackcurrant tea, and he sipped it. She poured out a pan of hot water and sprinkled yellow mustard flowers in it. Little Tim sat with his feet in the nice water, and the steam curled round his head, but still he sneezed.

'A-tishoo! A-tishoo!'

There came a knock at the door and the Hare looked in.

'What is the matter, Mrs Rabbit? I heard a very loud A-tishoo come from your house, and I saw the roof-thatch wobble. Is it safe?'

'Little Tim has caught a sneeze,' said Mrs Rabbit.

'Where did you find it, Tim?' asked the Hare.

'I found it out fishing,' said Tim, and his voice was croaky and muffled in the steam.

'Put a fur bandage round your throat,' said

Hare. He pulled some fur from his pocket. It was soft grey fur.

'Oh, thank you! Thank you,' said Mrs Rabbit. 'What a kind Hare you are!'

'I've been young myself, and I know about wet feet,' said the Hare. 'My son, Sam, comes home after fishing and this is how I cure his colds.'

Mrs Rabbit made the delicate fur into a bandage. She wrapped it round little Tim's neck. It was very comfortable and warm, but the tiny hairs tickled Tim's nose, and he sneezed more than ever.

'A-tishoo! A-tishoo!' went Tim.

The house shook and a bit of the ceiling fell down.

'Oh, dear me!' cried Mrs Rabbit, wringing her paws in dismay. 'I'm sure the house will tumble to bits if I can't stop Tim from sneezing.'

She put him to bed in the corner of the kitchen by the fire, but still he sneezed.

There came another knock at the door.

Tap, tap! Tap, tap! A Squirrel peeped in.

'Whatever is the matter, Mrs Rabbit? Such loud A-tishoos come from your house, my oak tree rustles. Is there anything wrong?'

'Oh, Miss Squirrel!' cried Mrs Rabbit, wiping her eyes on her apron. 'Tim has caught a sneeze. He can't get rid of it. I'm afraid it will blow the roof off. What shall I do?'

'Give him a dose of dandelion syrup, sweetened with honey,' said the Squirrel. 'I always take it when I have a cold.'

She put her paw in her bag and brought out a root of dandelion and a honeycomb.

'Oh, thank you! Thank you, Miss Squirrel!' said Mrs Rabbit. 'What a kind Squirrel you are!'

She made the dandelion syrup, and gave Tim a spoonful. It was very soothing to his throat, but he sneezed again.

'A-tishoo! A-tishoo!' he went, and the picture of 'Snow-White' fell from the wall with a clatter.

'Oh deary me!' cried Mrs Rabbit. 'Our best picture broken. The house will never stand the strain of this.'

She patted Tim and muffled him up, and put a log on the fire.

There came a tiny tap on the door. It was such a little tap it could hardly be heard, Tim was sneezing so loudly.

A Hen walked in, with little beak uplifted and wings fluttering anxiously.

'What is the matter, Mrs Rabbit?' she clucked. 'I was walking your way with my husband the Cock for company and I heard the A-tishoos. Is anything wrong?'

'Oh, Mrs Hen,' sighed Mrs Rabbit. 'My Tim has caught a sneeze, and he cannot get rid of it. I'm afraid it will blow our house down. What shall I do?'

'Give him an egg well beaten, and mixed with a pinch of poppy-dust,' said the Hen. 'I always take poppy-dust for a cold.'

She laid a brown egg on the floor, there and then.

'Oh, thank you! Thank you!' cried Mrs Rabbit. She broke the egg in a bowl and beat it to a froth with a twig and dropped a pinch of poppy-dust in it. Then she gave it to Tim.

He only sneezed the more.

'A-tishoo! A-tishoo!' he went, and the roof moved and shook.

There came a gentle push at the door and a Cow mooed softly outside.

'Whatever is the matter, Mrs Rabbit?' she lowed. 'The cattle are troubled by the loud A-tishoos coming from your cottage. Can I help you?'

'Oh, Mrs Cow, Mrs Mooley-Cow,' cried

Mrs Rabbit. 'My little Tim has caught a sneeze, and we cannot get rid of it. What shall I do?'

'Give him a mug of warm milk,' said the Cow. She stood still by the door while Mrs Rabbit milked her into a bowl.

'Oh, thank you! Thank you, Mrs Cow,' said Mrs Rabbit. 'What a kind Cow you are!'

She poured the warm frothy milk into Tim's own china mug, and held it out to Tim. He drank and he drank. He smiled happily, for he felt much better. Then suddenly he sneezed again.

'A-tishoo!'

It was such a loud sneeze that everybody and everything seemed to listen.

Tap! Tap-tap! Tap-tap-tap! Who was that at the door? Mrs Rabbit looked at Tim and Tim looked at Mrs Rabbit.

'Who's there?' called Mrs Rabbit.

Tap! Tap-tap! Tap-tap-tap!

The tip of a long red nose and white teeth came through the little door. It was the Fox himself.

'What is the matter, Mrs Rabbit?' he asked, in his smooth oily voice. 'I can get no peace for the loud A-tishoos that come from your house.'

'Oh, Mr Fox,' stammered Mrs Rabbit, and she was all of a tremble with fright. 'My little Tim has caught a sneeze, and it won't go. I'm very sorry, sir. I don't want to trouble you, sir. I'm afraid it will blow my roof off, and we shall have no home. What shall I do, sir?'

'Let me in, Mrs Rabbit. I'm a first-class doctor. I can cure any rabbit of a cold. Open the door very wide, so that I can get in.'

'Oh, no, Mr Fox,' said Mrs Rabbit, and she looked at Tim. Tim shook his head.

'I want to feel his pulse, poor Tim Rabbit,' said the Fox in a wheedling tone. 'I will drive that sneeze away.'

'Oh, no, Mr Fox,' said Mrs Rabbit stoutly. 'You might eat us, pulse and all. Oh, no, thank you. I would rather have the sneeze than the cure.'

'Just as you like, Mrs Rabbit. Keep your sneeze. I won't help you.' The Fox snorted angrily and went away.

Little Tim Rabbit sat up in bed, and his eyes were bright. He was so frightened that he quite forgot to sneeze. Then away out of the chimney flew that sneeze, and the house stopped shaking and the roof settled comfortably again on the timbers.

Little Tim Rabbit cuddled close to his mother and in a minute he was fast asleep. In the morning the cold had quite gone.

As for the sneeze, it climbed to the top of the fir tree, and there it lives, a-tishooing when the wind blows hard. You can hear it if you listen on a cold winter's night when you are safe in bed.

From *Adventures of Tim Rabbit* by Alison Uttley

The Rain

I hear leaves drinking rain;
  I hear rich leaves on top
Giving the poor beneath
  Drop after drop;
'Tis a sweet noise to hear
These green leaves drinking near.

And when the Sun comes out,
  After this Rain shall stop,
A wondrous Light will fill
  Each dark, round drop;
I hope the Sun shines bright;
'Twill be a lovely sight.

From *The Complete Poems of*
W. H. Davies

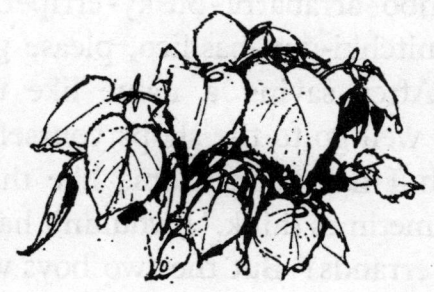

The Boy with the Long Name

ONCE upon a time there were two boys who were friends. They lived next door to each other and played together every day.

Now one of the boys had quite an ordinary name—he was called 'John'—but the other boy had a very special name. He was called 'Nicky-nicky-tembo-noso-rembo-arrabarra-busky-erriperido-hyti-ponpon-nitchki-don-basilico'.

Whenever anyone wanted a boy to run to the shops, it was always John who was asked, for it was much easier to say, 'John, please go to the shops,' than to say, 'Nicky-nicky-tembo-noso-rembo-arrabarra-busky-erriperido-hyti-ponpon-nitchki-don-basilico, please go to the shops.' After saying a name like that, you might as well go to the shops yourself.

'I wish I had a fine name like that,' John would sometimes think. 'I wouldn't have to run so many errands!' But the two boys were such good friends that they never quarrelled about it.

One day John fell into the well at the bottom of the garden. It wasn't very deep and there wasn't much water in it, but he couldn't get out by himself.

His friend (you remember his name?) ran off to the gardener and shouted, for the old man was rather deaf, 'JOHN HAS FALLEN INTO THE WELL.'

'All right! All right!' said the old man. 'There's no need to shout.' He fetched his ladder and helped John out of the well and the boy was no worse for his adventure.

A few days after this, Nicky-nicky-tembo-noso-rembo-arrabarra-busky-erriperido-hyti-ponpon-nitchki-don-basilico fell into the well.

John ran to the gardener for help. He began to shout: 'Nicky-nicky-tembo-noso-rembo...'

'Run away and play,' said the old man.

'But Nicky - nicky - tembo - noso - rembo - arrabarra-busky-erriperido-hyti-ponpon-nitchki-don-basilico has fallen into the well,' said John, very much upset. But the long name had taken so much breath to say that he had none left for the important part of his message.

'Go away!' said the old man. 'I've got work to do.'

John took a deep breath and shouted as quickly as he could, 'Nickynickytembonoso remboarrabarrabuskyerriperidohytiponponnitchkidonbasilico HAS FALLEN INTO THE WELL!'

'*Who's* fallen into the well?' asked the gardener. 'Oh, well, I suppose I'd better go and see.' So he fetched his ladder and went off grumbling, with John running ahead of him.

'Atishoo!' came from the well.

'Who's down there?' shouted the old man.

'Nicky-Atishoo! Nicky-Atishoo!' said the poor boy in the well.

'Never heard of him,' grumbled the old man, 'but I might as well pull him up, I suppose.'

So he did and there was poor Nicky-nicky-tembo - noso - rembo - arrabarra - busky - erri - perido - hyti - ponpon - nitchki - don - basilico, sneezing his head off. He had been in the well for such a long time that he was cold right through from his head to his toes. And all because of his very special name!

Well, his mother put him to bed and he was soon better again, but ever afterwards he was called 'Nicky'—just 'Nicky'—and a good thing too.

Anonymous

The Little Yellow Comb

JANE was just three years old, and she knew how to put on her own slippers, but she did *not* know how to comb her hair.

Everybody in the family helped to look after Jane, so everybody had a special comb for Jane's hair.

Her mother combed it with a white comb. Her aunt combed it with a big black comb. Her grandmother combed it with a long green comb, and her sister combed it with a little red comb. But Jane herself never combed it. She didn't know how.

'I want to comb my own hair,' said Jane.

'By and by you will be able to comb it,' said Mother.

'Want to comb it now,' said Jane.

'*Soon* you will be able to comb it,' said Mother.

One day Uncle Don came and took Jane for a walk and they looked in the shop windows.

'What would you like, Jane?' asked Uncle Don.

'A comb,' said Jane.

'What! A comb?' exclaimed Uncle Don.

'Yes, a comb—please,' said Jane.

Uncle Don couldn't think why Jane wanted a comb but he said, 'Of course you may have a comb.'

So they went into the shop, and when Jane saw a little yellow comb that she liked, Uncle Don paid the man for it and gave it to her. And when they got home Jane put the little yellow comb on the table by her bed.

The next day was Tuesday, and in the morning Jane began to comb her hair with the little yellow comb. She combed it up this way and down that way, and she combed it all ways, into a great big muddle.

Then her mother came in and said, 'Oh dear! Oh dear!' And her mother combed it straight.

The next day was Wednesday, and in the morning Jane began to comb her hair again with her little yellow comb. She began at the back and combed it so that it fell over her eyes and tickled her eyelids.

Then her aunt came in and said, 'Oh my!

Oh my!' And her aunt combed it straight.

The next day was Thursday, and in the morning Jane began to comb her hair again with the little yellow comb. She made a crooked parting at the back and a crooked parting on the top.

Then her grandmother came in and said, 'Oh, oh, my dear!' And *she* combed it straight.

And the next day was Friday, and in the morning Jane began to comb her hair again with the little yellow comb. She made a parting down the middle of the back and she combed her hair forward so that it curled round and over her ears and she couldn't hear when anybody called her.

But by and by Jane's sister came in and said, 'My goodness!' And *she* combed it straight.

The next day was Saturday.

In the morning Jane slipped out of bed

and when she had put on her slippers she stood before the mirror.

Then she picked up the little yellow comb and started combing—just *exactly* the way her mother and her aunt and her grandmother and her sister had done it, back over the top of her head and down to her neck, until when she had finished it looked smooth and tidy.

'Wonderful!' cried Jane's mother. 'Did you do that yourself?'

'Yes,' said Jane. And she smiled.

Then Jane's mother washed her white comb and put it away in a drawer. Her aunt washed her black comb and put it away in a drawer. Her grandmother washed her green comb and began to comb her own hair with it. And her sister washed her little red comb and put it away.

But Jane kept her little yellow comb that Uncle Don had given her and she combed her own hair with it—every day for always and always.

From *Ten Tales for the Very Young* by Marjorie Poppleton

The Little Woman's Water-Pot

EARLY one morning, a little African girl woke on her sleeping mat. She stretched and yawned when she heard her big sister, Deda, pounding maize into meal and singing. Zua wished she was big enough to pound maize. It sounded great fun.

But when Zua stood in the doorway of the round African house, she didn't look at her sister. No, she stared at Mboni, her mother, with unblinking round eyes, wondering whatever she could be making with so small a lump of clay.

'What do you make, Mama?' she asked curiously.

Mboni looked up.

'What do you think it is, my Brightness?'

Zua looked at the small lump of red clay in her mother's hands, wondering and wondering. Then she shook her curly head.

'It can't be a cooking-pot. It's far too small.'

'It's *not* a cooking-pot,' agreed Mboni, pressing her fist deep into the centre of the clay. Then she moulded the red clay into the shape of a jar with a narrow rim, turning and smoothing it with her strong, clay-stained hands.

'And it can't be a water-pot. It's far too small for that either,' said Zua.

Mboni laughed.

'But it *is* a water-pot, Zua. A little water-pot for a little woman.'

'She must be a very little woman if she can only carry a water-pot that size.' Zua sounded puzzled. 'I've never seen a woman as small as that, never.'

Deda laughed merrily.

'Ho! Ho! Just hark at Zua. She's never seen a little woman.'

Zua hated to be laughed at.

'Well, have you, Deda?'

'Oh, many, many times,' answered Deda, chuckling to herself as she gave the maize a final bang.

'Will you show me this little woman, Mama?' pleaded Zua, feeling very curious.

'If all goes well, you shall certainly know

her, my daughter,' promised Mboni gently, and with that Zua had to be content, for neither her mother nor sister would tell her any more about the little woman.

Soon Mboni set the tiny water-pot to dry in the sun. It looked very, very small beside the other water-pots and cooking-pots waiting to be baked.

'Don't touch the little water-pot, Zua. It is still very soft.'

As Mboni spoke, they heard Granny calling from her house not very far away.

'Mboni, Mboni, are you ready? It is time to fetch wood for the firing tomorrow.'

All the women of the village hurried off with hatchet, bush-knife and bark-string. Zua rode on her mother's back, for it was a long way to the forest.

'Why doesn't that little woman make her own water-pots, Mama?' whispered Zua in her mother's ear.

'She's far too small, Zua.'

'Is the little woman smaller than Deda?'

'Yes, much smaller. She can't even pound her own maize,' said Mboni. 'Now, Zua, see how big you can make your bundle of wood for the pot-firing.'

On the way home that afternoon, Zua had her own burden of wood to carry. She walked before her mother and sister proudly balancing it on her head without once touching it with her hands, just as they had taught her.

'Behold our little Brightness! Does she not bear her burden well?' said Mboni to Deda and their bright eyes gleamed with pride in their little one.

When all the wood had been placed round the firing-pit behind the village, Granny was satisfied. 'It is good!' she said. 'We have enough wood to fire many pots.'

Next morning while Mboni polished her unbaked pots with a pebble, Deda and Zua went to collect leaves for the firing-pit. It was great fun carrying huge banana leaves to use for lining the pit.

In the late afternoon when the sun was not so hot, Mboni called her daughters.

'Deda, Zua, it is time for the great firing. Come, help me to prepare the pots.'

The girls helped to pile the pots on top of each other, with leaves between each so that they should not be broken.

'I'll take the large cooking-pot,' said Mboni. 'Zua can carry the little woman's water-pot.'

'What, me?' asked Zua in great astonishment.

Mboni smiled.

'Yes, you, Zua. If you can carry wood you can carry water-pots, but be careful or the little woman will lose her water-pot before it is fired.'

Zua was careful, very careful. This was the first time she'd carried a water-pot on her head. It was much more difficult than carrying wood, for it might break if she let it drop.

'Look at Zua!' exclaimed Granny. 'Isn't she a clever girl!'

Zua glowed with delight and showed every one of her white teeth in a large smile, as she proudly walked through the village bearing her small burden.

Mboni placed the little woman's water-pot with the larger ones on the mound of leaves in the firing-pit. Then she helped Granny and the Aunts to fill all the pots with leaves and twigs and cover them with more leaves and wood. Then the large logs were piled into a high tower over the hidden pots. The time of firing had come!

Granny brought embers from her own fire in a broken crock and laid them on the dry leaves in the pit. The women knelt down and blew hard at the embers. The leaves spluttered, crackled and smoked, then out burst many flames at once. A lovely sight!

'The Great Fire is lit!' shouted the children, jumping up and down in their excitement.

But Zua sat quietly beside her mother, watching the flames. 'Please, fire, be kind to the little water-pot, make it hard, make it strong, to carry water for the little woman,' she said softly.

Soon even the big logs were blazing and the heart of the fire glowed like a furnace. It was so hot that the women and children had to draw back or the heat would have burnt them.

Tired with all the excitement, Zua fell asleep. When she awoke she saw her mother lifting a small pot out of the glowing mound of white wood-ash.

'The little woman's water-pot!' she shouted. 'Oh, do be careful, Mama!'

'Don't touch, Zua, it must cool first,' explained Mboni.

It seemed a long time to the little girl before her mother picked up the little water-pot and flicked it with her finger-nail.

'Ping! Ping!' sang the little water-pot.

'Hark, Zua!' said Mboni, flicking the little

water-pot again. 'Ping! Ping! It rings as true as a bell. It has fired perfectly. Not a crack, not a blister. It's the most beautiful water-pot I have ever made.'

'Won't the little woman be pleased!' cried Zua.

So a trail of women padded homewards on their hard-soled feet, each carrying a pile of newly-fired pots. But none was prouder than Zua carrying the little woman's water-pot on her own head.

Zua's father stood waiting at the door of their home.

'Well! Well!' he exclaimed. 'What a day for rejoicing! If it isn't the little woman, Zua, with her very first water-pot on her head. Welcome home, my own little woman!'

Then Zua's heart glowed with delight. At last she knew who the little woman was who was too small to make her own water-pot. It was herself!

Lilian Daykin

The Blackbird

In the far corner,
   Close by the swings,
Every morning
   A blackbird sings.

His bill's so yellow,
   His coat's so black,
That he makes a fellow
   Whistle back.

Ann, my daughter,
   Thinks that he
Sings for us two
   Especially.

From *Kensington Gardens*
by Humbert Wolfe

Mr Vinegar

MR AND MRS VINEGAR lived in a vinegar bottle. Now, one day, when Mr Vinegar was away from home, Mrs Vinegar, who was a very good housewife, was busily sweeping her house, when an unlucky thump of the broom brought the whole house clitter-clatter, clitter-clatter, about her ears. In an agony of grief she rushed forth to meet her husband. On seeing him she exclaimed, 'O Mr Vinegar, Mr Vinegar, we are ruined, we are ruined: I have knocked the house down, and it is all to pieces!'

Mr Vinegar then said: 'My dear, let us see what can be done. Here is the door; I will take it on my back, and we will go forth to seek our fortune.' They walked all that day, and at nightfall entered a thick forest. They were both very, very tired, and Mr Vinegar said: 'My love, I will climb up into a tree, drag up the door, and you shall follow.' He accordingly did so and they both stretched their weary limbs on the door, and fell fast asleep.

In the middle of the night, Mr Vinegar was disturbed by the sound of voices underneath, and to his horror and dismay found that it was a band of thieves met to divide their booty. 'Here, Jack,' said one, 'here's five pounds for you; here, Bill, here's ten pounds for you; here, Bob, here's three pounds for you.' Mr Vinegar could listen no longer; his terror was so great that he trembled and trembled, and shook down the door on their heads. Away scampered the thieves, but Mr Vinegar dared not quit his retreat till broad daylight. He then scrambled out of the tree, and went to lift up the door. What did he see but a number of golden guineas. 'Come down, Mrs Vinegar,' he cried; 'come down, I say;

our fortune's made, our fortune's made! Come down, I say.'

Mrs Vinegar got down as fast as she could, and when she saw the money, she jumped for joy. 'Now, my dear,' said she, 'I'll tell you what you shall do. There is a fair at the neighbouring town; you shall take these forty guineas and buy a cow. I can make butter and cheese, which you shall sell at market, and we shall then be able to live very comfortably.'

Mr Vinegar joyfully agrees, takes the money, and off he goes to the fair. When he arrived, he walked up and down, and at length saw a beautiful red cow. It was an excellent milker, and perfect in every way. 'Oh!' thought Mr Vinegar, 'if I had but that cow, I should be the happiest man alive.' So he offered the forty guineas for the cow, and the owner said that, as he was a friend, he'd oblige him. So the bargain was made, and he got the cow and he drove it backwards and forwards to show it.

By-and-by he saw a man playing the bagpipes—Tweedle-dum, tweedle-dee. The children followed him about, and he appeared to be pocketing money on all sides. 'Well,' thought Mr Vinegar, 'if I had but that beautiful instrument I should be the happiest man alive—my fortune would be made.' So he went up to the man. 'Friend,' says he, 'what a beautiful instrument that is, and what a deal of money you must make.'

'Why, yes,' said the man, 'I make a great deal of money, to be sure, and it is a wonderful instrument.'

'Oh!' cried Mr Vinegar, 'how I should like to possess it!'

'Well,' said the man, 'as you are a friend, I don't much mind parting with it; you shall have it for that red cow.'

'Done!' said the delighted Mr Vinegar. So the beautiful red cow was given for the bagpipes. He walked up and down with his purchase; but it was in vain he tried to play a tune, and instead of pocketing pence, the boys followed him hooting, laughing, and pelting.

Poor Mr Vinegar, his fingers grew very cold, and, just as he was leaving the town, he met a man with a fine thick pair of gloves. 'Oh, my fingers are so very cold,' said Mr Vinegar to himself. 'Now if I had but those beautiful gloves I should be the happiest man alive.' He went up to the man, and said to him: 'Friend, you seem to have a capital pair of gloves there.'

'Yes, truly,' cried the man; 'and my hands are as warm as possible this cold November day.'

'Well,' said Mr Vinegar, 'I should like to have them.'

'What will you give?' said the man; 'as you are a friend, I don't much mind letting you have them for those bagpipes.'

'Done!' cried Mr Vinegar. He put on the gloves, and felt perfectly happy as he trudged homewards.

At last he grew very tired, when he saw a man coming towards him with a good stout stick in his hand.

'Oh,' said Mr Vinegar, 'that I had but that stick! I should then be the happiest man alive.' He said to the man: 'Friend, what a rare good stick you have got!'

'Yes,' said the man; 'I have used it for many a long mile, and a good friend it has been; but if you have a fancy for it, as you are a friend, I don't mind giving it to you for that pair of gloves.' Mr Vinegar's hands were so warm, and his legs so tired, that he gladly made the exchange.

As he drew near to the wood where he had left his wife, he heard a parrot on a tree calling out his name: 'Mr Vinegar, you foolish man, you blockhead, you simpleton; you went to the fair, and laid out all your money in buying a cow. Not content with that, you changed it for bagpipes, on which you could not play, and which were not worth one tenth of the money. You fool, you—you had no sooner got the bagpipes than you changed them for the gloves, which were not worth one quarter of the money; and when you had got the gloves, you changed them for a poor miserable stick; and now for your forty guineas, cow, bagpipes, and gloves, you have nothing to show but that poor miserable stick, which you might have cut in any hedge.'

On this the bird laughed, and laughed, and Mr Vinegar, falling into a violent rage, threw the stick at its head.

Traditional

A Garage for Gabriel

THERE was once a little car whose name was Gabriel.

Now poor Gabriel had no garage. He lived out-of-doors on a piece of waste land where they sold used cars. He wore a sign that said, 'FOR SALE—CHEAP'.

There were dents in his bumpers. His paint was rusty. His doors sagged.

Every day Gabriel watched the shiny new cars roll by. But they never even looked at Gabriel.

'Oh,' thought Gabriel, 'how I should like to go whizzing right along. How I wish I were new and shiny!'

'But, specially,' he thought sadly, '*how* I wish I could have a garage!'

Well, one day two ladies came along.

They said to the man who sold cars, 'Have you a small car?'

He pointed to Gabriel.

'We'll try it,' they said. In they climbed.

'Now!' whispered Gabriel in great excitement. 'I'll show them I can whiz right along. Then the ladies will buy me and give me a garage.'

Whiz, whiz, whiz, went Gabriel round the streets.

He was feeling very happy.

Round and round the streets. *Whiz, whiz, whiz!*

'That will show them,' he thought.

But the ladies cried, 'Mercy, we don't want this car. It won't slow down at all.'

Gabriel felt very sad.

Next day a student came.

'Here's a fine car,' said the man.

'I'll try it,' said the student.

'Oh, ho!' thought Gabriel. 'This time I'll go very slowly, if that's what they want. Then the student will buy me and give me a garage.'

So he went v-e-r-y, v-e-r-y, v-e-r-y, s-l-o-w-l-y.

But the student said, 'That car is too slow!'

And off he marched.

Gabriel felt very sad.

But the next day a young lady came.

This time Gabriel was determined to do the right thing.

'I won't go too fast and I won't go too slow,' he said. 'But I'll show her I've got pep in my engine. Then she'll buy me and give me a garage.'

The young lady started the engine.

'BANG!' shouted Gabriel. 'BANG, BING, BANG, POP, POP!'

'My goodness!' cried the young lady. 'This car's much too noisy!'

And off she hurried.

'Oh, dear!' cried poor Gabriel. 'Won't *any-*

one ever buy me and give me a garage? I'll never be so noisy again!'

So the next day when a man came and pressed the starter, Gabriel didn't make any noise. Not *any* noise.

'This car won't even start,' said the man. He turned on his heel and left.

Well Gabriel felt just awful. Now he was sure that he never would have a garage.

And then Jimmy and Jimmy's daddy came along.

'Have you a car for sale?' asked Jimmy's daddy.

The man was so cross with Gabriel, he said, 'Yes—*there's* a car going cheap.'

'Let's buy it,' said Jimmy's daddy.

They climbed in.

Gabriel was so surprised that he didn't have time to show off. He just acted naturally.

They drove up the street and stopped in front of a little yellow house.

Then Jimmy's daddy greased Gabriel's engine till it purred like a pussycat.

'I sound very quiet!' thought Gabriel.

Then Jimmy's daddy hammered out the dents in the bumpers, and oiled the hinges and tightened up the sagging doors.

'Oh, I do feel good!' whispered Gabriel.

And last of all, Jimmy's daddy gave Gabriel a coat of shiny red paint.

'I look FINE!' shouted Gabriel.

Then Jimmy and his daddy and his mummy and Pooch, their cat, all went for a ride.

Every time they whizzed by another car, Gabriel bowed and smiled and the other cars bowed and smiled, too.

And when they came home, they whizzed right up the drive into a little, yellow garage!

From *Read Me Another Story* by Catherine Woolley

Safety First!

Leader: Look to the left,
Look to the right.
Is there a bus
Or a motor in sight?

Other children: Yes, I can see
A bus and a car.

Leader: Then we had better
All stay where we are.

Leader: Look to the left,
Look to the right.
Now is there anything
Coming in sight?

Other children: Left there is not,
Right there is not.
Both ways are clear.

All children: OVER WE TROT.

From *Adventures in Words* by Rodney Bennett

The Little Brown Egg

ONCE upon a time there was an old man, who liked nothing better than eggs. Every morning when the cock crew and the first birds sang, he put on his clothes and came downstairs. And in the yard, in the still grey light, he would call:

'Little brown egg, come fast, come soon,
And I'll eat you up with my silver spoon.'

And then he would look for a brown egg among the clucking hens.

'*Brown* eggs,' he said, 'are better than anything else in the world. Better than a jam-tart,' he said. 'Better than plum-cake, better than a gold watch, better than a new shirt.'

But the old man never found one. For every morning all the eggs were white. And it was always a white egg the old man put in his egg-cup and hit on the top with his old silver spoon.

Now one morning the birds sang early. And

instead of falling quiet again, while all the father and mother birds got breakfast ready as they generally did, they went on and on singing, as if it were already afternoon, or as if the sun had come out after rain.

So the old man knew it was a special day. He put on his clothes very carefully, and downstairs he went.

Out in the yard he called:

'Little brown egg, come fast, come soon,
And I'll eat you up with my silver spoon.'

And *this* time, he found a brown egg. It was deep, deep, brown, not the least bit speckled, and as round as a ball.

But when the old man went to pick it up, the brown egg rolled away. And as the old man went after it, it rolled faster and faster.

The old man ran after it, and as he ran, he called again:

'Little brown egg, come fast, come soon,
And I'll eat you up with my silver spoon.'

But the egg didn't stop.

The little brown egg rolled on and on till it came to a man cleaning windows. He rubbed and scrubbed them, and polished them round.

And they flashed and twinkled like lakes in the sun. But when he saw the brown egg rolling by, he dropped his bucket CRASH! And he dropped his duster SPLASH! And down from the ladder he jumped, and away after the little brown egg. And as he ran, he shouted:

'Little brown egg, come fast, come soon,
And I'll eat you up with my silver spoon.'

But the egg didn't stop.

It rolled and rolled, and the little old man and the window-cleaner ran as swift as birds after it. And by and by, it came to a postman.

The postman was taking letters to the houses with his fat, round bag.

'Clatter, clatter, clat!' went his hand through the letter-box. And 'Ratter, tatter, tat,' went his hand on the knocker.

But when he saw the egg come rolling by, he threw down his bag, and flung the letters up in the air. Up, up, they went like seagulls, and down they came like falling snow.

The postman ran after the egg, and as he ran he shouted:

'Little brown egg, come fast, come soon,
And I'll eat you up with my silver spoon.'

But the egg didn't stop.

And the little old man and the window-cleaner and the postman ran after it, as fast as the wind. By and by it came to some men mending the road.

One drove a steam-roller. One drove a tar-cart. One drove a stone-lorry, and two of them scattered stones. 'Pff,' went the tar, and the road was black. 'Tsss' went the stones, and the road was white. And 'blup-blup-blup' went the tall, wide steam-roller, clanging along, making everything firm and smooth.

But when the workmen saw the egg, they jumped down from their steering wheels, and threw down their shovels. And away over the hill went the steam-roller and the tar-lorry, and the cart full of stones, and nobody cared about them. And the pebbles went slithering down from their heap.

But the workmen ran after the little brown egg, and as they ran they shouted:

'Little brown egg, come fast, come soon,
And I'll eat you up with my silver spoon.'

But the egg didn't stop.

And the little old man and the window-cleaner, and the postman and the workmen ran after it, higgledy-piggledy. And at last it came to a railway-line.

Over the line puffed a passenger-train, swaying fast. 'Look out, look out!' shouted everyone. 'You'll all be run over.'

But when the engine-driver saw the little brown egg, he pulled on the lever and stopped the train. Then he wiped his hands on a piece of cotton-waste, and his fireman did the same.

And down they jumped, their faces as black as ink from the coal and smoke, and ran after the little brown egg. Right across the railway-line they ran, and all the passengers leaned out of the windows and called to them. And as they ran, they shouted:

'Little brown egg, come fast, come soon,
And I'll eat you up with my silver spoon.'

But the egg didn't stop.

The little old man, and the window-cleaner, and the postman and the workmen and the engine-driver and his fireman ran after it, crying and calling. But it rolled on and on till it came to a lake.

And as it trembled on the edge, a big fish opened his mouth.

'Plop,' went the egg.

'Snap,' went the fish.

And the little old man, and the window-cleaner, and the postman, and the four workmen, and the engine-driver, and his fireman lay down on the grass, in the tickly green grass, and stared into the water.

But though they looked and looked, through waves and ripples and fishes' tails, they never saw it again. So that must have been the end of the lovely little brown egg, that the old man had found on that special morning.

From *Lollipops* by Leila Berg

Charles and Jenny

'WILL you help me to put up the camp bed in your bedroom, Charles?' said his mother. 'Your cousin Jenny is coming to stay. She is four like you.'

As they spread the sheets and blankets on the little bed, Charles wondered what Jenny would be like. He had not seen her for so long that he could not remember anything about her.

'You will enjoy having someone to play with,' said Mother.

'Yes,' said Charles, though he did not look very pleased. 'She can play with my toys but she can't see what is in my USEFUL BAG. That's a secret.' His blue bag was slung over one shoulder and he gave it a pat and smiled. Only he knew what was inside.

Jenny came the next day. Charles thought she looked very nice. She had short, yellow plaits of hair tied with red ribbons. He showed her his toys in the cupboard and on the shelf and then she caught sight of the blue bag which he had hidden behind the brick-box.

'What do you keep in this big bag?' she asked and before Charles could stop her, she had opened the mouth of it and put in her hand.

'Leave my bag alone!' shouted Charles. 'It's my very own secret bag. Give it back!' And he snatched at the bag.

'I only wanted to have a look!' shouted Jenny, holding fast to the string.

Just then Mother came in to say that dinner was ready. Jenny let go of the string and Charles carried the bag into the dining-room and hung it on the back of his chair, while he ate.

After dinner Mother said to them, 'I have an idea for an indoor game as it is too wet for the garden. But I need two empty match-boxes, one each. And I can't find two anywhere. It is a pity.'

Charles smiled and opened his blue bag and fumbled about inside and brought out two empty match-boxes.

'What a useful bag!' said Mother. 'There's no guessing what's inside. Now this is the game. See how many tiny things you can collect in your match-box. But you must only have one of each kind. You can go where you like in the house.'

Charles was still a little bit cross. 'Jenny's match-box is bigger than mine,' he grumbled. 'It will hold more things.'

'Let's measure and see,' said Mother. So they laid one match-box on top of the other and they were exactly the same size.

Then Charles and Jenny ran off to look for tiny things to put in their match-boxes. They went everywhere, upstairs and downstairs, in and out of the bedrooms, in and out of the dining-room, in and out of the kitchen. They got out of breath with running and their cheeks were red and hot. Once they bumped into each other in the hall and they both laughed.

'I've found something else,' said Jenny, taking a pin off the pin-cushion.

'So have I,' said Charles, dropping a tiny glass bead into his match-box.

It would take too long to tell you all the things they managed to squeeze in. When Mother called, 'Time is up,' the lids would only just slide on, the boxes were so full. They emptied them out on the kitchen table and Mother counted. Jenny had twenty-five things and Charles had one less—he had twenty-four.

I will tell you some of Jenny's things: a piece of cotton, a cornflake, a feather, a button, a pin and a crumb.

Now I will tell you some of Charles' things: a match, a bead, a grain of rice, a stamp, a currant and a hair. The hair was a curly brown one. He had pulled it out of his own head.

Charles was not at all cross now. He did not mind Jenny having one more thing than he had.

'Do let's play it again,' said Charles. 'Can we go in the garden now the rain has stopped? Would you like to play it again, Jenny?'

'Yes, I would,' said Jenny.

'You can play it in the garden if you wear wellingtons,' said Mother. So they put on their wellingtons and ran outside.

There were not so many tiny things in the garden, but they collected petals and leaves and seeds and berries. When the time was up and Mother counted, Charles had twelve things and Jenny had eleven.

After tea, Charles opened his Useful Bag and told Jenny she could look inside if she wanted. It was half-full of things to keep other things in: there were tins and little bottles and match-boxes and screw lids.

'We might play shop with all these lovely things,' said Jenny.

'So we will, tomorrow,' said Charles. 'We will ask Mother to give us some real rice and tea and sugar to put in the jars.'

Charles was glad that Jenny had come to stay and was going to sleep in the camp bed in his room. Jenny was glad too.

From *Listen with Mother Tales* by Ruth Ainsworth

The Pretty Little Hen and Bad Mr Wolf

ONCE upon a time there was a Pretty Little Hen. She lived in a house by the Great Dark Forest.

In the forest lived Mr Wolf.

Now Mrs Hen, whenever she went out, looked this way and that way to see if Mr Wolf were anywhere around.

And as for Mr Wolf, whenever he went out, he, too, looked this way and that way, to see if Mrs Hen were anywhere around.

And WHY did Mr Wolf look round about him so?

He WANTED to see Mrs Hen so he'd make her into his dinner.

And WHY did Mrs Hen look round about her so?

She DIDN'T want to see Mr Wolf for *fear* he would make her into dinner.

So there they both were, forever seeking and hiding from each other.

But Mrs Hen got tired of looking this way and that way whenever she went out.

'Cluck, Cluck, Cluck; I will look for someone to live with me who will keep me safe from Bad Mr Wolf.'

And she chose a time when Bad Mr Wolf was out of the way and off she went towards the town to see whom she could find.

The first person she met was a Cow.

'Good day,' said the Cow. 'And where may you be going?'

'I am looking for someone to live with me to keep me safe from Bad Mr Wolf.'

'If I should come and live with you what will you give me?'

'I am not very rich and I have not much to give. But every morning for breakfast you shall have a fresh brown egg.'

But the Cow kicked up her heels and made the dust fly in Mrs Hen's face.

'Is that all you will give me? I don't like eggs. Not for MY breakfast.'

And this is true enough. What DO cows like for their breakfast?

Well, Pretty Mrs Hen went further along the road. And she met with a Dog.

'Good day,' said the Dog. 'And where may you be going?'

'I am looking for someone to live with me to keep me safe from Bad Mr Wolf.'

'If I should come and live with you what will you give me?'

'I am not very rich and I have not much to give. But every morning for breakfast you shall have a fresh brown egg.'

But the Dog began cutting capers to show how little he thought of it.

'Is that all you will give me? I don't like eggs. Not for MY breakfast.'

And this was true enough. What DO dogs like for their breakfast?

Well, Pretty Mrs Hen went further along the road. And she met with a Horse.

'Good day,' said the Horse. 'And where may you be going?'

'I'm looking for someone to live with me to keep me safe from Bad Mr Wolf.'

'If I should come and live with you what will you give me?'

'I am not very rich and I have not much to give. But every morning for breakfast you shall have a fresh brown egg.'

But the Horse started trotting up the road.

'Is that all you will give me? I don't like eggs. Not for MY breakfast.'

And this is true enough. What DO horses like for their breakfast?

Well, Pretty Mrs Hen went further along the road, and she met with a Cat.

'Good day,' said the Cat. 'And where may you be going?'

'I am looking for someone to live with me to keep me safe from Bad Mr Wolf.'

'And if I should come and live with you what would you give me?'

'I am not very rich and I have not much to give. But every morning for breakfast you shall have a fresh brown egg.'

The Cat looked very disgusted and ran up a tree.

'Is that all you will give me? I don't like eggs. Not for MY breakfast.'

And this is true enough. What DO cats like for their breakfast?

So Pretty Mrs Hen went further along the road. And she met with a Bee.

'He is not very big, but then he has got a sting. Bad Mr Wolf may be frightened of bees. Many people are,' thought Pretty Mrs Hen.

So when the Bee said 'Good day, and where

may you be going?' Mrs Hen answered: 'I am looking for someone to live with me to keep me safe from Bad Mr Wolf.'

'If I should come and live with you what will you give me?'

'I am not very rich and I have not much to give. But every morning for breakfast, you shall have a fresh brown egg.'

But the Bee disappeared into a flower and only his angry buzz could be heard.

'Is that all you will give me? I don't like eggs. Not for MY breakfast.'

And that is true enough. What DO bees like for their breakfast?

Poor Pretty Mrs Hen! She thought she would NEVER find anyone to live with her to keep her safe from BAD MR WOLF.

Just as she was turning home she saw a child.

'Hullo,' said the child. 'And where may you be going?'

'I am looking for someone to live with me to keep me safe from Bad Mr Wolf.'

'If I should come and live with you what would you give me?'

'That is just the trouble,' said poor Mrs Hen. 'I am not very rich and I have not much

to give, but every morning for breakfast you should have a fresh brown egg. But no one likes eggs for their breakfast. The Cow doesn't, the Dog doesn't, the Horse doesn't and the Cat doesn't, the Bee doesn't and I don't suppose you do.'

'Oh! Yes, I do!' said the child. 'That is JUST what I like for my breakfast.'

And that is true enough. Do YOU like an egg for your breakfast?

So the child went home and lived with Mrs Hen, and when Bad Mr Wolf came to hear of it:

'It's no good my staying around here. I shall never catch her now for my dinner,' he said.

And away he went and was never seen there again.

So Pretty Mrs Hen no longer looked this way and that way whenever she went out, and as for the child every day for breakfast there was

A FRESH BROWN EGG.

And IS that what you like for YOUR breakfast?

From *Nursery Tales* by Diana Ross

Blackie's Birthday

ONE day Jane said to her little black dog: 'Blackie, do you know that today is your birthday?'

'Woof!' replied Blackie, 'woof! woof!' and he jumped up and down, wagging not only his tail but almost the whole of his black, furry body.

'You're two years old today,' Jane told him.

'Woof! Woof!' said Blackie.

Then he stopped jumping up and down and began to sniff the air. 'Sniff! sniff!' he went, twitching his round black nose, which looked like a little piece of leather. 'Sniff, sniff!'

'He can smell his birthday present, Mummy,' laughed Jane, and she held more tightly a little parcel wrapped in brown paper.

Blackie put his nose on the parcel and then he tried to take it away in his mouth.

'No,' said Jane. 'No, Blackie. You mustn't snatch. Sit down. Sit.'

Blackie sat.

'Stay!'
Blackie stayed quite still. Jane put the parcel on the ground in front of him.
'All right!' she said. 'Open it!'
Blackie pulled the string off with his teeth. Then, making little growling noises, he bit the brown paper away, piece by piece. 'Gr . . . gr . . . gr . . .' he went, until all the paper was torn away. You would never guess what he found inside. It was something that was his

favourite thing to eat, something which he only had on his birthday or at Christmas. It was . . . *a cold sausage!*

No sooner had he found it than he gobbled it up just as fast as he could. Jane and her mother picked up the pieces of brown paper and string and threw them in the rubbish box.

'Blackie did enjoy his present,' smiled Mummy. 'As it's his birthday, I think he ought to do what he likes best of all, don't you?'

'And what he likes best of all,' said Jane, 'is going on the common and jumping into the pond.'

'Fetch your lead, Blackie!' said Mummy.

Blackie ran to the door where his lead hung from a hook. He pulled the lead from the hook and brought it to Jane and her mother so that they could fasten it to his collar. Then they all went out of the house and up the road towards the common.

As soon as they were away from all the cars and lorries and bicycles, Jane undid Blackie's lead and let him run. The first thing he did was to race as fast as he could towards the pond. 'Splosh! Splosh!' He was in the water. He swam across to the other side, and then he turned round and swam back again. By this time Jane and her mother had reached the pond and they saw him coming out of the water. He looked very small and thin because his fur was all stuck together. They ran a little way away so that he should not shake all the wetness over *them*!

Blackie shook himself and rolled on the grass to get dry. After they had walked a little farther, Jane said: 'I think Blackie would like to play hide-and-seek.'

'I'm sure he would,' Mummy agreed. 'You go and hide while Blackie and I shut our eyes.'

Mummy sat down beside Blackie and she held her hands over his eyes so that he could not see where Jane was running.

'Cuckoo!' called Jane. 'Cuckoo!'

Mummy took her hands away from Blackie. He looked first this way, then that way.

'Where's Jane?' Mummy asked him. 'Where's Jane?'

Blackie lifted his long ears and put his head on one side. He *loved* playing hide-and-seek.

'Where's Jane?' Mummy asked him.

Off he went, scurrying over the grass, looking first behind one tree, then behind another tree.

'Cuckoo!' cried Jane. 'Cuckoo!'

Her voice sounded quite near now. Blackie ran and looked behind a green bush and *there* was Jane. He was so pleased to see her that he almost knocked her down.

They played hide-and-seek for a long while. Sometimes Jane hid and sometimes Mummy hid. But Blackie always did the finding. He would not go away and hide by himself because he did not want to leave them.

That evening, after tea, Jane found a piece of blue ribbon which Mummy said she did not want. Jane put it through Blackie's collar and tied it in a bow.

'There!' she said. 'Now you're a birthday dog with a pretty bow.'

But Blackie didn't like the blue bow at all. He waggled his head and he waggled his neck until he could reach the bow with his mouth. Then he pulled it undone. Every time Jane made a nice new bow, Blackie untied it with his teeth. And then, at last, when Jane wasn't looking, he pulled it right off and chewed it into little pieces.

'Oh! Blackie!' said Jane.

'Never mind!' Mummy said, 'Blackie just doesn't feel comfortable in a bow. And I really think he's getting rather tired. Let's say good night to him before we turn on your bath water.'

Blackie was already creeping into his basket and curling himself into a ball. Jane patted his furry head. 'Good night, Blackie-dog,' she said softly.

Blackie opened one eye and gave a long, happy sigh. Ah-a-a-ah! What a day! He had had a cold sausage as well as his ordinary dinner. He had jumped into the pond. He had played hide-and-seek on the common. And he had torn a silly, blue bow into little pieces. He had had a *lovely* birthday.

From *A Story a Day* by Doris Rust

Who has seen the Wind?

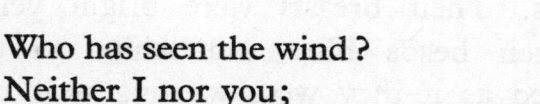

Who has seen the wind?
Neither I nor you;
But when the leaves hang trembling
The wind is passing through.

Who has seen the wind?
Neither you nor I;
But when the trees bow down their heads
The wind is passing by.

Christina Rossetti

A Spring Story

THERE were once two tiny birds, called Bluetits. Their breasts were bright yellow and their heads blue and white so that it looked as if they were wearing neat blue caps.

Mr and Mrs Bluetit lived in a big garden. There were insects for them to eat and sometimes they would find a juicy piece of fat or a piece of coconut hanging from a tree. What they liked best were monkeynuts and they swung to and fro, upside down, pecking at the shells until they found the sweet nuts. 'This garden is a fine place to live,' they said, 'there is so much to eat.'

Then one day spring came. Blue and white flowers came out in the garden and the sun shone more warmly every day. 'It is quite time we built our nest,' said Mrs Bluetit.

'Let's try the wood first,' suggested Mr Bluetit and the two birds flew busily amongst the trees, peeping into hollows in the bark and chinks in the wall. But all the holes were too small or too damp or too large. 'Sparrows might get in—nasty creatures sparrows are!' said Mr Bluetit.

At last they found just the right place, a bird's nesting-box on the fence. It had a little round hole for a front door and it was warm and dry inside. Mrs Bluetit was very pleased. 'Now we can begin,' she said.

'You find some moss in the wood,' she said to her husband, 'and I'll look near the house. Perhaps there will be something useful there.'

And so there was—she found some scraps of soft wool and some tiny feathers, just the thing for lining a nest.

At last the nest was finished. 'How soft and warm this will be for my babies,' thought little Mrs Bluetit.

Next day she laid one egg and each day after that she laid one more. Now seven tiny white eggs marked with reddish spots filled the nest. Mrs Bluetit settled down to keep the eggs warm while Mr Bluetit flew to a branch nearby and sang a tinkling song because he was happy.

Time went by and one day Mrs Bluetit heard a noise in the nest. *Tap, tap! Tap, tap!*

It was the baby birds pecking at their shells. One by one, seven tiny birds came out of their shells. They were too young to have any feathers, but they all had wide-open beaks! Mr Bluetit gave one look inside the nest at his seven hungry children, then flew away in a hurry to find food for them.

All day he carried insects and dropped them into the little birds' mouths. Mrs Bluetit helped him but it was very hard work feeding seven children. At the end of the day Mr and Mrs Bluetit were tired out.

Day by day the little birds grew stronger and soon they were covered with soft downy feathers. They had grown so big that the nest was very crowded. The strongest bird climbed on top of his brothers and sisters. 'I'm going to get out,' he shouted.

'Oh no, you're not!' scolded his mother. 'You must wait until we are all ready. It won't be long now.'

Very early one morning, Mr Bluetit called to his children to get ready to leave the nest. 'Just follow me—don't be afraid,' he said.

He popped out of the front door and the bravest little bird followed him. When he saw the big garden and what a long way it was to the ground, even he felt a little frightened. Next moment his brothers and sisters pushed him so hard that he flopped down on to the grass. Soon all the little birds were safely out of the nest.

'Come along all of you, try your wings!' said Mr Bluetit and they followed him to a branch nearby. There they sat, making an excited squeaky sound, but they weren't still long. Soon they were flying all over the garden finding good things to eat and chasing each other for fun.

'Keep away from the rough starlings,' warned Mrs Bluetit, but the little birds were enjoying themselves too much to listen.

Early next day, the seven little birds flew away over the wall to find new adventures outside the garden. They never came back again to that garden, and no one knows where they went. Perhaps some of them came to your garden?

Vera Colwell

Henrietta and the Cows

HENRIETTA was looking for someone who might be a good friend for her. It was not easy. She was walking along the bottom of a ditch at the side of the road. She was afraid the Bad People might see her and want to cook her up and eat her. She was creeping along ever so quietly, when she was seen by an old man resting on a milestone. In his hand he held a long thick stick. He stretched out and stopped Henrietta by poking her in the chest with the end of the stick. 'Oh!' she exclaimed.

'Hello, little hen,' said the old man, staring curiously down at her. 'Why are you hiding in that wet and muddy ditch?'

'W-w-well,' shivered Henrietta, backing away and looking fearfully at the stick, 'm-m-m-my friends t-told me this great wide world was f-full of B-Bad P-People who would c-c-c-c-cook me up and eat me.'

'Nonsense,' replied the old man, 'there are lots of people who wouldn't want to eat a nice hen like you. Look at those cows in the meadow there. They're a fine lot. Very quiet and gentle. You go and speak to them, and see. Mark my words, little hen, you'll find lots of people in this great wide world who wouldn't want to harm one of your little white feathers.'

Henrietta, encouraged by the old man's words, climbed out of the muddy ditch, and crossed the field to where the cows stood in a group. They were all bent over the thick green grass, munching with their big square teeth. They were such huge creatures, with big fat tummies, and long sharp horns sticking out of their heads, Henrietta was afraid they would rush at her when they saw her and stamp her under their hooves. But they didn't. In fact they took no notice of the little white hen, as she came bravely trotting up.

'Hello!' said Henrietta brightly. 'I'm Henrietta, and I was wondering if I could stay with you, if you don't mind.'

The cow nearest to her looked up and stared at our hen with her big cowy eyes. Then she turned to the cow next to her and said, 'Mooo'.

The second cow looked up. 'I'm Henrietta,' the little hen quickly said to her, 'and I'd like to stay in this nice meadow with you if you don't mind.'

The second cow stared at Henrietta with her big cowy eyes. After a while she said, 'Mooo'.

Henrietta now looked around and saw all the other cows staring at her with their big cowy eyes. 'I'm Henrietta,' said she, 'I have no home, and I'd like to stay here and live with you if you don't mind.' And the other cows replied one after the other:

'Mooo.'
'Mooo.'
'Mooo.'
'Mooo.'
'Mooo.'
'Mooo.'
'Mooo.'
'Mooo.'
'Mooo.'

Then all together they said:
'Moooooooooooooooooooooo.'

Then they lowered their heads to the grass again and began to munch. They moved slowly down the meadow, and Henrietta followed

them. She was quite pleased with them, because they did not try to harm her. The kind old man was right. The cows were a pretty decent lot. But it would be nice if they could stop munching the grass for a while and say, 'Hello'. Henrietta could tell them about her life on the farm, and they could tell her about life in the fields and meadows. But they moved along all in the same direction, munching the grass without saying a word. And it looked to our little hen as she followed behind as if they were going to carry on munching all day.

Suddenly she had an idea. She always made the other hens in the farmyard laugh by dancing about and saying nursery rhymes. She would make the cows laugh by reciting *Little Jack Horner*. She scampered around to face them, and, hopping comically from one leg to the other, began to recite:

'Little Jack cluck! Horner,
Sat in the cluck! corner,
Eating his puck-cluck!-mas pie,
He put in his thumb,
And pulled out a pluck! plum,
And said, "What a puck-cluck! boy am I!"'

Then she bowed and purposely fell on her back. It really was a most amusing performance. But the cows looked at her gloomily with their big cowy eyes. One of them said, 'Mooo'. The others replied, 'Mooo'. 'Mooo'. 'Mooo.' 'Mooo.' 'Mooo.' 'Mooo.' 'Mooo.' 'Mooo.' 'Mooo.' Then they all together said, 'Moooooooooooooooooooooo'.

Henrietta stamped her foot. She was getting very fed up with them. 'Cows! Cows!' she cried. 'Can't you say anything but "Mooooo" ?'

'Mooooo,' they replied.

'Stop saying, "Mooooo"!' shouted the angry little hen. 'Say anything, but don't say, "Mooooo"!'

'Mooooo,' they replied.

'If you say "Mooo" again,' shrieked Henrietta, 'I'll go away and never come back!'

'Mooooo,' they replied.

So Henrietta furiously turned her back on them and flounced out of the meadow. And when she was walking down the road again she heard them for the last time:

'Mooooooooooooooooooooo.'

Well, thought our little white hen, as she walked on, I could have stayed with those cows quite comfortably. They had a very gentle manner. But what could we talk about all day? Mooooooo! Mooo! Mooo! Mooo! Mooo! Moooooooooooooooooooo! Why, in a week I'd go dotty!

From *The Adventures of Henrietta Hen* by Aaron Judah

Henny-Penny

ONE day Henny-penny was picking up corn in the cornyard when—whack!—something hit her upon the head. 'Goodness gracious me!' said Henny-penny; 'the sky's a-going to fall. I must go and tell the king.'

So she went along and she went along and she went along till she met Cocky-locky. 'Where are you going, Henny-penny?' says Cocky-locky.

'Oh! I'm going to tell the king the sky's a-falling,' says Henny-penny.

'May I come with you?' says Cocky-locky.

'Certainly,' says Henny-penny. So Henny-penny and Cocky-locky went to tell the king the sky was falling.

They went along, and they went along, and they went along, till they met Ducky-daddles. 'Where are you going to, Henny-penny and Cocky-locky?' says Ducky-daddles.

'Oh! We're going to tell the king the sky's a-falling,' said Henny-penny and Cocky-locky.

'May I come with you?' says Ducky-daddles.

'Certainly,' said Henny-penny and Cocky-locky. So Henny-penny, Cocky-locky, and Ducky-daddles went to tell the king the sky was a-falling.

So they went along, and they went along, and they went along, till they met Goosey-poosey. 'Where are you going to, Henny-penny, Cocky-locky, and Ducky-daddles?' said Goosey-poosey.

'Oh! We're going to tell the king the sky's a-falling,' said Henny-penny and Cocky-locky and Ducky-daddles.

'May I come with you?' said Goosey-poosey.

'Certainly,' said Henny-penny, Cocky-locky, and Ducky-daddles. So Henny-penny, Cocky-locky, Ducky-daddles, and Goosey-poosey went to tell the king the sky was a-falling.

So they went along, and they went along, and they went along, till they met Turkey-lurkey. 'Where are you going, Henny-penny, Cocky-locky, Ducky-daddles, and Goosey-poosey?' says Turkey-lurkey.

'Oh! We're going to tell the king the sky's a-falling,' said Henny-penny, Cocky-locky, Ducky-daddles, and Goosey-poosey.

'May I come with you, Henny-penny, Cocky-locky, Ducky-daddles and Goosey-poosey?' said Turkey-lurkey.

'Oh, certainly, Turkey-lurkey,' said Henny-penny, Cocky-locky, Ducky-daddles, and Goosey-poosey. So Henny-penny, Cocky-locky, Ducky-daddles, Goosey-poosey and Turkey-lurkey all went to tell the king the sky was a-falling.

So they went along and they went along, and they went along, till they met Foxy-woxy, and Foxy-woxy said to Henny-penny, Cocky-locky, Ducky-daddles, Goosey-poosey and Turkey-lurkey: 'Where are you going, Henny-penny, Cocky-locky, Ducky-daddles, Goosey-poosey and Turkey-lurkey?'

And Henny-penny, Cocky-locky, Ducky-daddles, Goosey-poosey and Turkey-lurkey said to Foxy-woxy: 'We're going to tell the king the sky's a-falling.'

'Oh! But this is not the way to the king, Henny-penny, Cocky-locky, Ducky-daddles, Goosey-poosey, and Turkey-lurkey,' says Foxy-woxy; 'I know the proper way; shall I show it you?'

'Oh, certainly, Foxy-woxy,' said Henny-penny, Cocky-locky, Ducky-daddles, Goosey-poosey, and Turkey-lurkey. So Henny-penny, Cocky-locky, Ducky-daddles, Goosey-poosey, Turkey-lurkey, and Foxy-woxy all went to tell the king the sky was a-falling.

So they went along, and they went along, and they went along, till they came to a narrow and dark hole. Now this was the door of Foxy-woxy's cave. But Foxy-woxy said to Henny-penny, Cocky-locky, Ducky-daddles, Goosey-poosey, and Turkey-lurkey: 'This is the short way to the king's palace: you'll soon get there if you follow me. I will go first and you come after, Henny-penny, Cocky-locky, Ducky-daddles, Goosey-poosey, and Turkey-lurkey.'

'Why, of course, certainly, without doubt, why not?' said Henny-penny, Cocky-locky, Ducky-daddles, Goosey-poosey, and Turkey-lurkey.

So Foxy-woxy went into his cave, and he didn't go very far, but turned round to wait for Henny-penny, Cocky-locky, Ducky-daddles, Goosey-poosey, and Turkey-lurkey. So first Turkey-lurkey went through the dark hole into the cave. He hadn't got far when 'Hrumph,' Foxy-woxy snapped off Turkey-lurkey's head and threw his body over his left shoulder.

Then Goosey-poosey went in, and 'Hrumph,' off went her head and Goosey-poosey was thrown beside Turkey-lurkey.

Then Ducky-daddles waddled down, and 'Hrumph,' snapped Foxy-woxy, and Ducky-daddles was thrown alongside Turkey-lurkey and Goosey-poosey.

Then Cocky-locky strutted down into the cave, and he hadn't gone far when 'Snap, Hrumph!' went Foxy-woxy, and Cocky-locky was thrown alongside of Turkey-lurkey, Goosey-poosey and Ducky-daddles.

But Foxy-woxy had made two bites at Cocky-locky, and when the first snap only hurt Cocky-locky, but didn't kill him, he called out to Henny-penny. But she turned tail and off she ran home, so she never told the king the sky was a-falling.

Traditional

Just Like Me

First Child: I went up one pair of stairs
Second Child: *Just like me.*
                I went up two pairs of stairs
                Just like me.
                I went into a room
                Just like me,
                I looked out of a window
                Just like me,
                And there I saw a monkey
                Just like me.

                                  Anonymous

Galldora and the Rooks

ONE wild, windy day Galldora, the rag doll, was swung up into the air by Marybell. Up and up the wind carried Galldora, but she never came down, for Galldora fell *plump* into an old rooks' nest. It was a thin old nest full of holes, and the rag doll settled right in the middle. Galldora looked down and far below she saw the grass like a green sea, and Marybell far, far away.

'Oh!' said Galldora to herself. 'Now what will become of me?'

'Never mind, Galldora,' called up Marybell, 'the twigs will soon break in the wind and you'll come falling down. I'll go away and have my tea now and come back for you later.'

But Marybell forgot to come back. Anyway it would have been no good, for the twigs held and Galldora remained stuck in the old rooks' nest.

Next day two rooks came and looked at the rag doll.

'Aaaah!' said one.

'Aaaah!' said the other.

'Oh, go away, rooks,' said Galldora. 'Don't bother me. This is my home now and I'm happy here.'

But the two rooks started pulling Galldora about. One pulled her arms while the other pulled her feet. But as they were both pulling in different ways, Galldora stayed where she was.

At last the rooks gave up. They hopped from branch to branch, flapping their wings and looking again at the rag doll. They looked at her this way, then they looked at her that way. Then one rook looked at her from above, and the other rook looked at her from below.

One rook called, 'Floor.'

'Aaaah!' called the other, nodding its head. 'Floor-floor.'

They flew away, still calling 'Floor-floor' to each other.

What do they mean? Galldora asked herself. She soon found out. They made her into a floor and built a new nest on top of her. After a few days she was covered with twigs, and only her head stuck up in the middle.

After a few more days there were five eggs in the nest. The mother rook sat on the eggs to keep them warm. When she flew off to find food Galldora kept the eggs warm with her wool hair.

One sunny day out of the five eggs, with a peck-peck, came five baby rooks.

'Aaaah! Aren't my babies bonny?' called the mother rook proudly.

If I was asked, said Galldora to herself, I would say I had never seen such ugly babies.

But though Galldora thought they were ugly, she took a great liking to the baby rooks, and she began to feel motherly towards them.

At first she did not like the way they pecked her eyes and pulled at her hair, but she got used to it.

Then, after a while, the baby rooks grew so big that the nest seemed very crowded and much too small.

'I do wish they wouldn't sit on my head,' said poor Galldora.

One night, the wind started to blow. It blew in a wild way, and it bent and shook the high tree and the rooks' nest. The father and mother rook became very worried. They kept calling 'Aaaah-aaaah!' to each other.

Whatever happens, said Galldora to herself, very firmly, I must not fall down, for if I fall the nest will come down too, and then what will happen to the baby rooks? And yet, added Galldora sadly, I would like to fall down. I am getting very tired of being up here. The baby rooks have grown so big, and the nest is getting very stuffy. Still, I must not be selfish and think about myself.

As the wind blew out the night stars and then blew in the dawn the rag doll began to feel very strange. Her legs had fallen down and only her arms held up the nest.

'Listen, baby rooks,' she said. 'Sit on my

arms and head, so that when I fall down you can float down with me.'

The baby rooks did as Galldora said. With the last wild gust of wind, Galldora fell, and the baby rooks, sitting on her, floated down. They fell on a soft flower-bed, Galldora first and the baby rooks on top of her.

The mother rook and the father rook were so happy that their babies were safe, they gave Galldora a couple of sharp pecks with their beaks and said, 'Aaah-aah!' in a thank-you way.

The baby rooks were calling, 'We can fly'. And they started right away flapping their wings, and taking little flops from here to there. Soon they were all safe on a low May-tree.

Later Marybell found Galldora. She gave her a hug and said, 'Why, Galldora, wherever have you been? I've been looking for you everywhere and I thought you were really lost for good this time.' Marybell had quite forgotten that she had left Galldora in the tall tree.

From *The New Adventures of Galldora* by Modwena Sedgwick

Elephant Big and Elephant Little

ELEPHANT BIG was always boasting.

'I'm bigger and better than you,' he told Elephant Little. 'I can run faster, and shoot water higher out of my trunk, and eat more, and . . .'

'No. You can't!' said Elephant Little.

Elephant Big was surprised. Elephant Big was *always* right. Then he curled up his trunk and laughed and laughed.

'What's more, I'll show you,' said Elephant Little. 'Let's have a running race, and a shooting-water-out-of-our-trunks race, and an eating race. We'll soon see who wins.'

'I shall, of course,' boasted Elephant Big. 'Lion shall be judge.'

'The running race first!' Lion said. 'Run two miles there and two miles back. One of you runs in the field, the other one runs in the forest. Elephant Big shall choose.'

Elephant Big thought and thought, and Elephant Little pretended to talk to himself: 'I hope he chooses to run in the field, because *I* want to run in the forest.'

When Elephant Big heard this, he thought: 'If Elephant Little wants very much to run in the forest, that means that the forest is best.' Aloud he said: 'I choose the forest.'

'Very well,' said Lion. 'One, two, three. Go!'

Elephant Little had short legs, but they ran

very fast on the smooth springy grass of the field.

Elephant Big had long, strong legs, but they could not carry him quickly along through the forest. Broken branches lay in his way; thorns tore at him; tangled grass caught at his feet. By the time he stumbled, tired and panting, back to the winning post, Elephant Little had run his four miles, and was standing talking to Lion.

'What ages you've been!' said Elephant Little. 'We thought you were lost.'

'Elephant Little wins,' said Lion.

Elephant Little smiled to himself.

'But I'll win the next race,' said Elephant Big. 'I can shoot water much higher than you can.'

'All right!' said Lion. 'One of you fills his trunk from the river, the other fills his trunk from the lake. Elephant Big shall choose.'

Elephant Big thought and thought, and Elephant Little pretended to talk to himself: 'I hope he chooses the river, because *I* want to fill my trunk from the lake.'

When Elephant Big heard this, he thought: 'If Elephant Little wants very much to fill his trunk from the lake, that means the lake is best.' Aloud he said: 'I choose the lake.'

'Very well!' said Lion. 'One, two, three. Go!'

Elephant Little ran to the river and filled his trunk with clear, sparkling water. His trunk was small, but he spouted the water as high as the trees.

Elephant Big ran to the lake, and filled his long, strong trunk with water. But the lake water was heavy with mud, and full of slippery, tickly fishes. When Elephant Big spouted it out, it rose only as high as a middle-sized thorn bush. He lifted his trunk and tried harder than ever. A cold little fish slipped down his throat, and Elephant Big spluttered and choked.

'Elephant Little wins,' said Lion.

Elephant Little smiled to himself.

When Elephant Big stopped coughing, he said: 'But I'll win the next race, see if I don't. I can eat much more than you can.'

'Very well!' said Lion. 'Eat where you like and how you like.'

Elephant Big thought and thought, and Elephant Little pretended to talk to himself: 'I must eat and eat as fast as I can, and I mustn't stop; not for a minute.'

Elephant Big thought to himself: 'Then I must do exactly the same. I must eat and eat as fast as I can, and I mustn't stop; not for a minute.'

'Are you ready?' asked Lion. 'One, two, three. Go!'

Elephant Big bit and swallowed, and bit and swallowed, as fast as he could, without stopping. Before very long, he began to feel full up inside.

Elephant Little bit and swallowed, and bit and swallowed. Then he stopped eating and ran round a thorn bush three times. He felt perfectly well inside.

Elephant Big went on biting and swallowing, biting and swallowing, without stopping. He began to feel ever so funny inside.

Elephant Little bit and swallowed, and bit and swallowed. Then again he stopped eating, and ran round a thorn bush six times. He felt perfectly well inside.

Elephant Big bit and swallowed, and bit and swallowed, as fast as he could, without stopping once, until he felt so dreadfully ill inside that he had to sit down.

Elephant Little had just finished running round a thorn bush nine times, and he still felt perfectly well inside. When he saw Elephant Big on the ground, holding his tummy and groaning horribly, Elephant Little smiled to himself.

'Oh, I do like eating, don't you?' he said. 'I've only just started. I could eat and eat and eat and eat.'

'Oh, oh, oh!' groaned Elephant Big.

'Why, what's the matter?' asked Elephant Little. 'You look queer. Sort of green! When are you going to start eating again?'

'Not a single leaf more!' groaned Elephant Big. 'Not a blade of grass, not a twig can I eat!'

'Elephant Little wins,' said Lion.

Elephant Big felt too ill to speak.

After that day, if Elephant Big began to boast, Elephant Little smiled and said: 'Shall we have a running race? Shall we spout water? Or shall we just eat and eat?'

Then Elephant Big would remember. Before very long, he was one of the nicest, most friendly elephants ever to take a mud bath.

From *Elephant Big and Elephant Little* by Anita Hewett

The Engine Driver

The train goes running along the line,
   Jicketty-can, jicketty-can.
I wish it were mine, I wish it were mine,
   Jicketty-can, jicketty-can.
The Engine Driver stands in front,
He makes it run, he makes it shunt.

   Out of the town,
   Out of the town,
   Over the hill,
   Over the down,
   Under the bridges,
   Across the lea,
   Over the ridges
   And down to the sea.

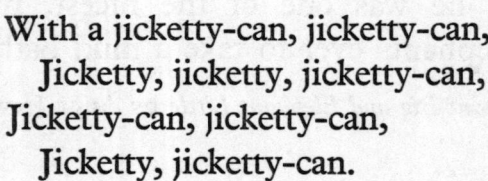

With a jicketty-can, jicketty-can,
   Jicketty, jicketty, jicketty-can,
Jicketty-can, jicketty-can,
   Jicketty, jicketty-can.

     From *Speech Rhymes* edited by Clive Sansom

Jane and the Hair Wave

ONE day it was Mother's birthday. Jane had a shilling to spend on a present for her. So she sat down to think what she could buy that Mother would like. Then she remembered that Mother often said to her, 'Oh, Jane, what straight hair you have. I wish it would curl.'

So Jane got off her chair and went out of the front door, down the street and round the corner to the hairdresser.

When she got into the shop she saw the hairdresser waving a lady's hair. Jane had to wait until he had finished. Then she said to him: 'Will you please curl my hair for one shilling?'

And the hairdresser said, 'Certainly, Madam. Just step this way, please.'

Jane went into a cubicle behind a curtain, she sat down in the chair in front of a big looking-glass and a basin.

'First, I shall have to wash your hair,' the hairdresser said.

He put a lot of soapy water on Jane's hair and rubbed it very hard. Then he rubbed it with a towel, and last he blew hot air at it with a drying machine.

'Now,' he said, 'I will wave the hair, Madam.'

He took out two pairs of curling tongs, and he waved Jane's hair all over till it was as curly as a lamb's coat. Then Jane paid him her shilling and ran home.

When she got to the front door she found it was shut, so she rang the bell. Mother opened the door and looked at Jane.

'Who are you,' asked Mother, 'and what do you want?'

'I am Jane,' said Jane, 'and I want to come in.'

'Oh no, you can't be Jane,' said Mother, 'because my Jane has straight hair, and you have very curly hair. I don't know where Jane is, but I am quite sure you are someone else.'

Poor Jane was very sad at this, and she said to Mother, 'Don't you like my curly hair?'

'I am sure it is very pretty,' Mother said, 'but you see my Jane has straight hair, so I like that best.'

Jane turned round and ran all the way back to the hairdresser's shop. When she got there she said to the hairdresser, 'Please will you uncurl my hair at once?'

So the hairdresser washed Jane's hair all over again and all the curls disappeared. When her hair was quite dry Jane got up to go, and the hairdresser said, 'As the wave was not satisfactory, Madam, I shall be pleased to refund your shilling.'

And he gave Jane back her shilling. Jane thanked the hairdresser and then she went into the sweet shop next door and bought some bullseyes and some acid drops. When she had got them, she went home and rang the front door bell again. When Mother opened the door she said: 'Oh Jane, I am glad to see you.'

'Here is a birthday present,' said Jane, and she gave Mother the bullseyes and the acid drops.

'How lovely!' Mother said. 'Thank you very much, darling. Let's each have one now.'

While they were sucking the sweets, Jane said: 'Did someone come to see you today?'

'Yes,' Mother said, 'a funny little girl with fuzzy hair, who said she was Jane, but I knew she couldn't be because of her hair.'

'Don't you wish that I had curly hair, then?' asked Jane.

'No,' said Mother, 'I like my Jane with straight hair best.'

From *Stories for Jane* by Catherine Storr

Puss and Pup

ONCE upon a time Puss and Pup kept house together. They had their own little cottage in the wood. Here they lived together and tried to do everything just like real grown-up people. But somehow they couldn't always manage this. You see, they had small clumsy paws, without any fingers like people have, only little soft pads with claws on them. So they couldn't do everything just like real grown-ups. And they didn't go to school, because school is not meant for animals.

Of course it isn't. School is only for children.

Their home was not always as tidy as it might have been. Some things they did well, and others not so well. And sometimes there was rather a mess.

One day they noticed that the cottage floor was very dirty.

'I say, Pup,' said Puss, 'our floor's horribly dirty. Don't you think so?'

'Yes, I do. It really is rather dirty,' said

Pup. 'Just look how grubby it's made my paws.'

'They're filthy,' said Puss. 'Ugh, you ought to be ashamed of yourself! We must scrub the floor. People don't have dirty floors. They scrub them.'

'All right,' replied Pup. 'But how are we going to do it?'

'Oh, it's easy,' said Puss. 'You go and fetch some water, and I'll see to the rest.'

Pup took a pail and went for water. Meanwhile Puss took a piece of soap out of her bag and put it on the table. Then she went off to the box-room for something; I expect she kept a piece of smoked mouse there.

While she was away Pup came back with the water and saw something lying on the table. He unwrapped it. It was pink.

'Ha, ha! This looks good,' said Pup to himself. And because it made him feel hungry, he pushed the whole piece into his mouth and started chewing it.

But it didn't taste so good. Soon Puss came in and heard Pup making all sorts of funny spluttering noises. She saw that Pup's mouth was full of foam and his eyes were streaming with tears.

'Goodness me!' cried Puss. 'Whatever's happened to you, Pup? You must be ill. There's foam dripping from your mouth. Whatever's the matter?'

'Well,' said Pup, 'I found something lying here on the table. I thought it might be some cheese, or a piece of cake, so I ate it. But it stings horribly and makes my mouth all full of foam.'

'What a silly you are!' scolded Puss. 'That was soap! Soap's for washing with, not eating.'

'Oh,' said Pup. 'So that's why it hurts so much. Ow, ow, it stings, ow, it stings!'

'Have a good drink of water,' suggested Puss; 'that'll stop it smarting.'

Pup drank away until he had finished up all the water. It had stopped smarting by now, but there was still plenty of foam. So he went and wiped his muzzle on the grass outside. Then he had to go and fetch some more water because he had drunk it all and there was none left. Luckily Puss had a shilling, and she went off to buy some more soap.

'I won't eat that again,' said Pup, when Puss returned with the soap. 'But, Puss, how are we going to manage without a scrubbing brush?'

'I've already thought about that,' said Puss. 'You've got a rough, bristly coat, just like a brush. We can scrub the floor with you.'

'Right ho!' said Pup. And Puss took the soap and the pail of water, and knelt down on the floor. Then she scrubbed the whole floor with Pup.

By now the floor was all wet, and it wasn't any too clean either.

'We ought to rub it over with something dry,' said Puss.

'I'll tell you what,' said Pup. 'I'm sopping wet, but you're dry, and your fur is nice and soft. It'll make a lovely floor-cloth. I'll dry the floor with you.'

So he took hold of Puss and dried the whole floor with her.

The floor was now washed and dried, but Puss and Pup were all wet and terribly dirty from having been used to wash the floor.

'Well, we do look a sight!' they both said, looking at each other. 'We've got the floor clean all right, but now look at us! We can't possibly stay like this. Everybody will laugh. We'll have to be sent to the wash.'

'Let's wash each other, like they do at the

laundry,' said Pup. 'You wash me and when I'm done, I'll wash you.'

'Very well,' said Puss.

They filled the tub of water and took a scrubbing-board. Pup got into the tub and Puss washed him. She rubbed him so much on the scrubbing-board that Pup begged her not to press so hard, as his legs were getting all tangled up.

When Pup was finished, Puss got into the tub and Pup scrubbed and squeezed her so much that she begged him not to press her so hard on the scrubbing-board in case he made a hole in her fur.

Then they wrung each other out.

'Now we'll hang ourselves out to dry,' said Puss. So they put out the clothes-line.

'First you hang me up on the line, and when I'm up, I'll get down and hang you up,' Pup told Puss.

So Pup took hold of Puss and hung her up, just like washing. They didn't need any pegs, because they could hold on to the line with their claws. Once Puss was on the line, she jumped down and hung up Pup.

By now the two of them were hanging nicely and the sun was shining brightly.

'The sun's shining on us,' cried Pup. 'We'll soon be dry.'

No sooner had he said this than it began to rain.

'Oh, dear, it's raining!' shouted Puss and Pup. 'The washing will get wet. Let's take it down!'

They jumped down quickly and ran to the cottage for shelter.

'Is it still raining?' asked Puss.

'It's stopped,' said Pup, and sure enough the sun was out again.

'Let's hang the washing out again, then,' said Puss.

So they hung themselves on the line a second time. First Pup put Puss up, and as soon as she was hanging up, she jumped down and put up Pup. So they both hung on the line, just like washing, and were very pleased at the way the sun shone and made such a good drying day.

But then it began to rain again.

'It's raining! Our washing will get wet!' cried Puss and Pup. And they ran for shelter. Soon the sun came out again, and again they hung each other up on the clothes-line. Then it started raining, and off they scampered.

Then the sun came out again and they hung themselves up again, and so it went on till the evening. By that time they were both quite dry.

'Our washing's dry,' they said. 'Let's put it in the basket.'

So they clambered into the basket. But then they felt so sleepy that they both fell asleep. And they slept in the basket right through until the next morning.

From *Harum Scarum* by Josef Căpek, translated by Stephen Jolly

The Old Woman and her Pig

AN old woman was sweeping her house, and she found a little crooked sixpence. 'What,' said she, 'shall I do with this little sixpence? I will go to market, and buy a little pig.'

As she was coming home, she came to a stile: but the piggy wouldn't go over the stile.

She went a little further, and she met a dog. So she said to him 'Dog! Dog! bite pig; piggy won't go over the stile; and I shan't get home tonight.' But the dog wouldn't.

She went a little further, and she met a stick. So she said: 'Stick! Stick! beat dog, dog won't bite pig; piggy won't go over the stile; and I shan't get home tonight.' But the stick wouldn't.

She went a little further and she met a fire. So she said: 'Fire! Fire! burn stick; stick won't beat dog; dog won't bite pig; piggy

won't go over the stile; and I shan't get home tonight.' But the fire wouldn't.

She went a little further, and she met some water. So she said: 'Water! Water! quench fire; fire won't burn stick; stick won't beat dog; dog won't bite pig; piggy won't go over the stile; and I shan't get home tonight.' But the water wouldn't.

She went a little further, and she met an ox. So she said: 'Ox! Ox! drink water; water won't quench fire; fire won't burn stick; stick won't beat dog; dog won't bite pig; piggy won't go over the stile; and I shan't get home tonight.' But the ox wouldn't.

She went a little further, and she met a butcher. So she said: 'Butcher! Butcher! kill ox; ox won't drink water; water won't quench fire; fire won't burn stick; stick won't beat dog; dog won't bite pig; piggy won't go over the stile; and I shan't get home tonight.' But the butcher wouldn't.

She went a little further; and she met a rope. So she said: 'Rope! Rope! hang butcher; butcher won't kill ox; ox won't drink water; water won't quench fire; fire won't burn stick; stick won't beat dog; dog won't bite pig; piggy won't go over the stile; and I shan't get home tonight.' But the rope wouldn't.

She went a little further, and she met a rat. So she said: 'Rat! Rat! gnaw rope; rope won't hang butcher; butcher won't kill ox; ox won't drink water; water won't quench fire; fire won't burn stick; stick won't beat dog; dog won't bite pig; piggy won't go over the stile; and I shan't get home tonight.' But the rat wouldn't.

She went a little further, and she met a cat. So she said: 'Cat! Cat! kill rat; rat won't gnaw rope; rope won't hang butcher; butcher won't kill ox; ox won't drink water; water won't quench fire; fire won't burn stick; stick won't beat dog; dog won't bite pig; piggy won't go over the stile; and I shan't get home tonight.' But the cat said to her: 'If you will go to the cow, and fetch me a saucer of milk, I will kill the rat.' So away went the old woman to the cow.

But the cow said to her: 'if you will go to the hay-stack and fetch me a handful of hay, I'll give you the milk.' So away went the old woman to the hay-stack; and she brought the hay to the cow.

As soon as the cow had eaten the hay, she gave the old woman the milk; and away she went with it in a saucer to the cat.

As soon as the cat had lapped up the milk, the cat began to kill the rat; the rat began to gnaw the rope; the rope began to hang the butcher; the butcher began to kill the ox; the ox began to drink up the water; the water began to quench the fire; the fire began to burn up the stick; the stick began to beat the dog; the dog began to bite the pig; the little pig in a fright jumped over the stile: and so the old woman got home that night.

Traditional

Tails

Cows' tails go swishing about,
Cats' tails are twirly,
Wasps' tails have very sharp stings,
Lambs' tails are nice little things,
And pigs' tails are curly.

Anonymous

At the Seaside

STEPHEN and Janet were going to the seaside.

The day before they set out, their mother gave them a red woollen bag. 'This is for your toys,' she said. 'You can take whatever you like with you to the seaside, as long as it will fit in this bag.'

'I *must* take my boat,' said Stephen. He had a small toy boat with a mast and a sail and a flag which he often sailed in the paddling pool in the park.

'I can't go without Polly,' said Janet. Polly was a tiny old-fashioned wooden doll her Granny had given her. Polly wore a striped cotton dress and her black hair was painted on her wooden head.

The children spent a happy afternoon looking at all their toys and choosing what to take with them. They put in all kinds of things and each of them took a favourite book. Janet chose *Squirrel Nutkin*—because he sailed across a lake, she said.

'But he sailed on a *leaf*!' said Stephen. 'I'm going to take my *Robinson Crusoe*, the one with lots of pictures, then I shall know what to do if my boat gets wrecked on a desert island.'

Next day the journey to the sea seemed long because each member of the family was so eager to get there, but at last they saw the shining sea and heard the sound of the waves.

Early next morning, Stephen and Janet went to buy their buckets and spades. Janet chose a blue one, Stephen a red one and they raced down to the beach to dig and make sand-pies.

It was a lovely hot day. The sun shone all the time. The children on the beach ran in and out of the warm water, Stephen and Janet with them. Janet collected pretty pebbles and shells and Stephen sailed his boat.

Wherever Janet went, Polly went too. The little doll lived in Janet's pocket when she had one, and in the toy-bag when she hadn't. At night Polly slept on Janet's pillow.

One day the children made a big sand-castle, with their father to help them dig. There was quite a deep moat round it and Stephen sailed his boat there.

'I say, Janet,' he said. 'Let's have Polly as the captain of the boat.'

'She'll fall off into the water,' objected Janet.

'Oh no, she won't. I'll fasten her to the mast with a rubber band.' Stephen ran off to look in the toy-bag for his box of odds and ends. Sure enough, there was a rubber band there, so he fastened the little doll firmly to the mast. The boat looked much more real with someone on board.

But after a time the tide began to go down and the water drained out of the moat. 'I'll sail my boat in the sea,' said Stephen, tired of playing with the sand-castle.

'Give me Polly back first,' said Janet.

'No,' said Stephen crossly, 'I want her for crew,' and he ran off, Janet after him. Into the sea he splashed and began to sail his boat.

'Don't let Polly sail away,' cried Janet anxiously.

'Of course not, silly,' said Stephen—he was still cross. 'I'm holding the string so the boat can't get away.'

But just then an unexpectedly big wave rolled in. Stephen, caught unawares, lost hold of the string and the boat was washed away from him with the tide.

'Oh, what will happen to Polly!' cried Janet.

She tried to wade towards the boat but the water was too deep for her short legs. Stephen realised that he couldn't reach the boat either.

Janet began to cry. 'Polly will never come back,' she sobbed.

'Run and fetch Daddy,' said Stephen. 'I'll stop here—perhaps someone will come along to help.'

Jane ran off across the sands while Stephen tried to keep his eyes on the little boat, but it wasn't easy.

Then he saw a boy swimming not far away. 'Hi!' he called. 'Oh, please will you catch my boat.'

The boy turned his head and made a grab at the boat, but he missed it and it sailed on. 'Sorry!' he shouted. 'Too far out for me, but I'll try to keep an eye on it.'

Stephen was almost in tears. He knew it was his fault that Janet might lose her doll and he his boat. But here was his father running across the beach and behind him Janet and his mother.

'Show me where the boat is, Stephen,' said his father. 'It's so small that it's difficult to spot unless you know where to look.' Stephen pointed and the boy waved and called. Stephen's father waded out into the water and began to swim.

'Oh, I do hope that Daddy's in time to stop it going out to sea,' said Stephen anxiously. 'It might sail right over to America!'

'Will Polly be safe?' asked Janet, holding her mother's hand tightly.

'I think so, darling,' said her mother comfortingly. 'Daddy's a very good swimmer.'

Stephen's father had to swim quite a long way, for the tide was running out fast, but suddenly he saw the little boat bobbing about almost under his nose, its flag still fluttering bravely from the mast and Polly safe on deck.

'Got it!' he shouted, seizing the trailing string, and he turned and began to swim back towards the shore.

By this time several children were watching with Stephen and Janet excitedly. 'Hooray! Hooray!' they shouted when Stephen's father waded out of the water.

'I'm sorry, Janet,' Stephen whispered, his face rather red, but Janet was looking at Polly. She was quite safe, but her dress was wet through and some of her hair had washed off in the sea.

'Polly's dress is spoilt, Mummy,' she said.

'Well, it was quite time she had a new one,' said her mother. 'I think I've got a stripey handkerchief with me which would be just right for her. Just think what a lot Polly will have to tell the other dolls when she gets home! It's not every doll that has sailed out to sea and nearly got wrecked.'

'No, but Polly is special,' said Janet, hugging the little doll.

'And so is my boat,' said Stephen. 'It sailed jolly well!'

'Dinner-time!' said his mother. 'Come along, all of you. What an adventure!'

Eileen Colwell

Cuckoo!

FOR his fifth birthday, Tim was given a cuckoo clock. It was a wooden clock with white numbers painted on its face, and two white hands that pointed to the time. Below the clock hung a long chain with a weight on the end. All day long, and all night too, it swung to and fro; *tick-tock, tick-tock, tick-tock*. But the best thing about Tim's cuckoo clock was this: every hour, a little door opened above the clock face, and out popped a tiny wooden cuckoo.

'*Cuckoo! cuckoo! cuckoo!*' he called, as many times as there were hours in the day.

Daddy hung the cuckoo clock on the wall in Tim's bedroom. Each morning at seven o'clock the little wooden bird popped out and sang seven '*Cuckoos!*' to let Tim know that it was time to wake up. In summer, when the sun shone through the window-pane and the sycamore tree outside waved its green, leafy boughs, Tim used to leap up at once. It seemed

a shame to lie in bed. But in winter, when silver frost patterned his window-pane, and the branches of the sycamore tree were bare, Tim liked to snuggle down inside his warm cosy bed, and not get up until Mummy called, 'Breakfast's ready!' Then he would jump out of bed, fling off his striped pyjamas, get washed, brush his teeth, put on his clothes, and comb his spiky yellow hair all in the most tremendous hurry. And *helter-skelter, crash-bang-wallop* he would run downstairs.

'You really must get up earlier, Tim,' his mother would tell him in a scolding voice.

But I am afraid Tim did not take any notice; he stayed in bed longer and later each winter day.

In January, Tim started school. He had a brand-new satchel, a shiny black paint-box, and a set of red pencils with his name stamped on them in gold letters: TIMOTHY. After breakfast each morning, he would leave the house and walk to the bus stop at the corner of the street, where he got the school bus with all the other boys and girls. The bus set off at half-past eight. Tim liked going to school. There were letters and numbers to learn about, plasticine to play with, and in one corner of the classroom there was a model shop, where the children took turns to buy and sell things, using cardboard pennies, sixpences, and shillings. Best of all, Tim found out how to tell the time! Now he knew how many hours and minutes the hands of his cuckoo clock were pointing to. The little hand was the hour hand. It crept slowly past the numbers on the clock face. The big hand was the minute hand. It ran quickly past the numbers. They told the time together.

But although he enjoyed going to school, Tim was still very lazy about getting out of bed each morning. Sometimes he was so late that he had to run to catch the school bus in time.

On the first day of spring, Tim woke as usual at seven o'clock, when the little wooden cuckoo called to him seven times. He rumpled his spiky yellow hair with one hand and yawned and stretched.

'Mmnmmn—I needn't get out of bed for ages!' he thought, and he pulled the bedclothes over his ears.

Daddy came up and knocked on Tim's door.

'Time to get up, Tim!' he called.

But Tim stayed right where he was.

Mummy was busy in the kitchen. A smell of sizzling bacon, frying eggs, and warm toast came wafting up the stairs and squeezed itself under Tim's door.

'Breakfast's ready!' Mummy called.

And still that lazy boy did not get out of bed.

'I shan't get up until my cuckoo calls out eight times!' he told himself.

And at that very second, the little doors flew open above the clock face, and out popped the tiny cuckoo.

'*Cuckoo! cuckoo! cuckoo! cuckoo! cuckoo! cuckoo! cuckoo! cuckoo!*' he called.

'Eight o'clock,' thought Tim. 'Now I will get up!'

But what do you think happened? The cuckoo gave *another* call: '*Cuckoo!*'

This gave Tim a dreadful shock. 'It's *nine* o'clock!' he wailed. 'I've missed the bus! What shall I do? Oh crumbs, oh crumpets, oh dear, oh dear!'

He never thought of *looking* at the clock.

He jumped right out of bed, out of his striped pyjamas, whizzed along to the bathroom, and squeezed his sponge on to his hands and face. He seized his vest and pants, his shorts and shirt and jersey, socks and shoes, and put them on in such a hurry that his shirt was back-to-front, and his shoes ended up on the wrong feet. He pulled his comb through his spiky hair, then dashed downstairs *helter-skelter-bang-wallop*!

'No time for breakfast!' he cried as he rushed through the kitchen. 'I'm late for school!' And he ran straight out of the back door.

Mummy and Daddy were eating their eggs and bacon. They stared at each other in astonishment, their knives and forks half-way to their mouths, as Tim banged the kitchen door.

Down the road ran Tim. He turned the corner—and there was the bus, still waiting for him! He leapt on board and flopped into a seat, blowing and puffing. After a moment he looked round. That was funny! There was no one else on the bus at all; he was quite alone. Tim wondered what had happened to all the other children.

At that moment the bus driver appeared. He was a jolly man with ginger whiskers.

'Hallo, sonny,' he said when he saw Tim. 'You're early today!'

'I'm *late*, you mean,' Tim said.

The bus driver looked at his wrist-watch. 'It's only ten minutes past eight,' he said.

'Ten minutes past *nine*, you mean,' said Tim.

'It must be ten minutes past nine, because my cuckoo clock called out nine times, and it never makes a mistake!'

'Doesn't it now?' the bus driver said. 'Are you quite sure about that?'

'Of course I am!' Tim told him. Then he remembered something. 'The last *cuckoo* did sound a bit different from the other eight,' he said, 'now I come to think of it.'

The bus driver threw back his head and roared with laughter. 'That was a *real* cuckoo you heard calling the ninth time!' he said. 'I heard it myself this morning. Listen! If we keep quiet we may hear it again.'

Tim and the bus driver stayed quite still and listened carefully. Yes—there it was! Away in the distance they heard '*Cuckoo!*' and then 'Cuckoo!' again.

And in the topmost branch of the sycamore tree outside Tim's bedroom window, there perched a clumsy big brown bird—the real live cuckoo! For it was the first day of spring.

And after that morning, I am happy to say that Tim never got up late again.

From *A Story to Tell* by Barbara Ker Wilson

The Magic Seeds

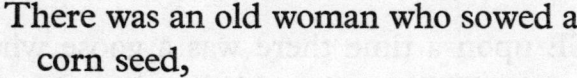

There was an old woman who sowed a corn seed,
And from it there sprouted a tall yellow weed.
She planted the seeds of the tall yellow flowers,
And up sprang a blue one in less than an hour.
The seed of the blue one she sowed in a bed,
And up sprang a tall tree with blossoms of red.
And high in the treetop there sang a white bird,
And his song was the sweetest that ever was heard.
The people they came from far and from near,
The song of the little white bird for to hear.

From *The Blackbird in the Lilac* by James Reeves

Honk Honk!

ONCE upon a time there was a goose whose name was William, but his mother, Mother Goose, always called him Willie.

'Now, go for a waddle, Willie,' she would say, 'and honk to the other geese.'

Willie was very fond of honking!

'Honk honk!'
'Honk honk!'
'Honk honk!'
'Honk honk!'

he went as he waddled along.

One day, when he was going for a waddle, he met a cat. It was a lovely black cat with two white paws in front. Willie was pleased.

'Honk honk!' he said to the cat. 'Honk honk!'

'Mieow!' said the cat.

Willie was surprised. 'What does "mieow!" mean?' he thought. He thought that cats said, 'Honk honk!' just like geese.

He waddled a bit further and nibbled at the

grass. It was a lovely day. The sun was shining and all the birds were singing.

'Honk honk!' said Willie.

'Bow wow!' barked a dog that was trotting along the road.

'Neigh!' said the milkman's horse. And 'Gee up!' said the milkman.

Poor Willie couldn't understand a thing.

Just then a farmer passed by. 'Hallo, goose!' he said.

'Honk honk!' said Willie.

Then some children passed. And one little boy came up to him and said, 'Boo!'

Willie was upset. He felt quite down in the beak.

'I know I'm a goose,' he thought. 'But they needn't say "Boo!" to me like that.'

Presently he saw a goldfish swimming in a pond, but however loudly he honked to it the goldfish just swam round and round and took no notice of him.

He waddled a bit further and met some cows.

'Moo!' they said. 'MOOOOO! MOOO!'

Then he met some hens.

'Cluck cluck cluck,' they said, 'cluck cluck cluck!' And the cock said 'Cockadoodledooo!'

'Oh, I wish someone would say "Honk

honk!" to me,' thought Willie. 'I feel so lonely!'

Some pigeons cooed and ducks quacked and the crows in the treetops cawed. But no one at all, *no one* said 'Honk honk!' to him.

Poor Willie began to cry and tears ran down his beak and fell with a splash at his pretty pink feet. 'Honk honk!' sobbed Willie.

Then from a long way away, he heard, 'Honk honk! Honk honk! Honk honk!'

What a beautiful sound!

He looked up and there, coming down the road, was a little blue motor car.

'Honk honk!' it went. 'Honk honk!'

'HONK HONK!' said Willie, 'HONK HONK!'

'HONK HONK!' went the car as it passed.

Willie gazed after it.

He *was* a happy goose.

'Honk honk!' went the car, disappearing round the corner.

'Honk honk!' said Willie.

From *Another Time Stories* by Donald Bisset

Rat-a-Tat-Tat

Question: Rat-a-tat-tat!
 Who is that?
Answer: Only grandma's pussy cat.
Question: What do you want?
Answer: A pint of milk.
Question: Where's your money?
Answer: In my pocket.
Question: Where's your pocket?
Answer: I forgot it.
 Oh, you silly pussy cat!

Traditional London Street game

The Old Red Bus

NOT so very long ago an old red bus ran down to the station and back again. It was a rumbling, grumbling bus. It was a rusty and dusty bus. It was a jumping, bumping bus. And because it was all these things some people walked to the station rather than rode in the old bus. It bumped and shook them about too much.

'The trouble with this bus,' the driver said, 'is that it is worn out. It needs a new engine to drive it. It needs new tyres to make it run along without bumps. It needs new seats and new windows and new paint—in fact I think we need a new *bus*!'

Now the old red bus wasn't at all surprised to hear this. It did feel worn out. Climbing hills made its engine work so hard the old bus thought surely it would one day fall to pieces. Changing gears and shouting 'honk-honk' at every corner made it feel tired too. So all the old red bus wanted to do was to sleep in the sun for ever.

'UR-UR-UUUURRR!' it grumbled. 'Since I'm so worn out there is no need for me to go another wheel turn.'

But while it was saying this, inside the bus the conductor was calling out, 'Fares, please! Fares, please!' He sold pink tickets from his machine to passengers, and their money dropped into his black bag with a tinkling plink, plink, plink!

And inside the bus the driver was sitting in his front seat in front of the wheel. He pushed the gear into place. He pulled off the brake and before the old bus knew what was happening it was rolling off down the road again.

'UUUUUrrr-UUUUUrrrr-UUUUUrrrr!' the old bus grumbled and mumbled. 'Gggrrr! I'm too tired to go another wheel turn!'

And to its surprise, the old red bus didn't.

Just then it ran over a piece of wood dropped on the road.

'SSSSSSSSSSS!'

The front tyre on the old red bus felt very funny. '*Sssss!*' It felt as though it was shrinking smaller and smaller. What was happening to its plump, round sides? The front tyre on the old red bus was as flat as a piece of paper.

'Oh, my front tyre!' gasped the old red bus very much surprised.

And the driver stopped the bus and jumped out. The bus conductor jumped out. All the people poked their heads out through the windows.

'The front tyre is as flat as a pancake,' the driver told the people, 'and since we can't repair it here I think you had better walk to the station.'

'We'll get the mechanic from the garage,' the bus conductor told them.

So all the people climbed out of the red bus and looked at a big nail in the piece of wood that had made the hole in the tyre and let out all the air, '*sssssss*'.

Shaking their heads all the people said, 'This is too bad. What we need is a new bus.' Off they walked to the station.

When the mechanic came with his box full of tools he tapped the old red bus with a spanner and said, 'This bus needs more than a new tyre.'

'Yes,' the driver answered. 'It's just about worn out. What we need is a new bus. Could you sell us a new bus?'

'Not today,' the mechanic said shaking his

head, 'but in a couple of weeks we could make this old bus as good as new at the garage.'

Everyone thought this was a wonderful idea —even the old red bus. So when the break-down van came the bus helped as much as it could. The break-down van had a crane on its back. The crane lifted the front wheels of the bus away, away off the ground. With just its two back wheels on the road the old red bus ran along behind the break-down van all the way to the garage.

Some people saw the old red bus being towed away and they said to one another, 'It looks as though we will be getting a new bus after all. The old bus must be going to the scrap-heap!'

At the garage the mechanics took out all the worn parts of the engine and put in new parts. They gave the bus a huge meal of oil and grease. They gave the bus new tyres and new seats. Then they gave the bus a new coat of sparkling red paint. The old bus didn't feel old any longer. It felt like running a thousand miles or two; up hills, down hills and along lumpy, bumpy roads.

When the time came for the red bus to drive along the road to the station everyone wanted a ride. All the people crowded in and said, 'This *isn't* the old rumbling, grumbling bus! Surely this couldn't be the old dusty, rusty bus! Don't tell us this is the old bumpy, jumpy bus!'

But we know it was, don't we?

From *Listening Time* by Jean Chapman

About
Mr MacPherson's Ducks

ONE morning in summer Mr MacPherson started his big red truck, and drove it down the hill and along the valley and over the next hill to the market.

At the market there were lots of people. Some farmers came with animals to sell and some farmers came to buy animals.

Mr MacPherson went along all the yards where the animals were waiting. He didn't want to buy any big brown-eyed cows. He didn't want to buy any woolly sheep. He didn't want to buy a galloping horse or a little white goat or a fat pig with black spots on it.

Mr MacPherson wanted to buy some ducks to swim on the water in his dam. The dam had a pump, and a windmill, and tadpoles in it, but—no ducks.

At last Mr MacPherson saw a tall man unloading a wooden crate from a truck, and in the trucks were—ducks.

They were very straight up and down white ducks, and they had shiny yellow beaks and shiny yellow feet and shiny black eyes.

'Please will you sell me those ducks,' said Mr MacPherson to the tall man.

'Yes,' said the tall man. 'There are ten of them and they are all quite young. If you make them a nest of straw, and feed them with plenty of mash and green thistles they will lay beautiful big eggs every day.'

Mr MacPherson gave the tall man the money and the tall man put the crate of ducks in the back of Mr MacPherson's big red truck.

'The two smallest ducks are called Mamie and Semolina,' said the tall man quite sadly. 'Mamie is the one with a black feather in her tail.'

'I'll remember,' said Mr MacPherson, and he started up the big red truck, 'DRM-ERM-RRM' and drove back to his farm.

He put the ten white ducks in a nice little house with wire on the front and straw on the floor and a big bowl of fresh drinking water.

'Tomorrow,' he said, 'I shall let you out in the paddock. You can swim on the dam, or walk down the lane in the long grass, but whatever you do DON'T GO IN THE ORCHARD.'

So the next morning after he had fed the ducks with plenty of bran and pollard and green thistles, he opened the door and all the ducks came waddling out, one after the other in a straight line.

Six white ducks went to swim in the dam and chase tadpoles.

Two white ducks went to walk in the long grass and catch grasshoppers. But Mamie and Semolina, the two smallest white ducks, were very, very naughty.

They went to the orchard and squeezed themselves under the gate.

They caught snails and caterpillars and ate some apples they found. Then they looked away through the rows of apple trees and there was a beautiful patch of fresh green grass—the greenest they had ever seen.

Mamie and Semolina began to run. They ran right into the middle of the soft green grass, right up to their shiny black eyes. And then . . . and then they found it wasn't grass at all. It was nasty sticky weed which people call Tailor's Needle because it has thin fine little leaves. It was as sticky as toffee or honey or jam. It stuck all over Mamie and Semolina.

They were sticky on their beaks, and sticky on their eyes. All down their lovely white necks, on their wings and tails and legs and yellow feet Mamie and Semolina were STICKY.

They struggled out of the green patch after quite a long time.

They ran along the dusty track that led to the gate. As they flapped their feet along the ground the black dust puffed up like a cloud. It stuck on the sticky stuff that the weed had left, and very soon Mamie and Semolina were black from head to foot.

By the time they found their way back to the duck house Mr MacPherson was spooning a big bucketful of mash to the other ducks.

When he saw Mamie and Semolina he called, 'Go away you two black ducks. You don't belong to me.'

Mamie and Semolina stopped. They didn't know what to do.

'Go on! Shoo!' said Mr Macpherson, waving his wooden spoon at them. 'All my ducks are lovely white ones with yellow beaks and yellow feet, but you are ugly black ducks with black

beaks and black feet. You'd better go back to wherever you came from.'

Mamie and Semolina had a good idea. They waddled over to the water trough and dipped their black sticky beaks in the clear water. They shook the water off the end of their beaks, and little drops of water flew up like a shower. The water rolled down their black faces and dripped on their black feet.

They looked as if they were crying, but the water washed little clean places in the sticky black dirt! Mr MacPherson looked hard and he saw patches of white and yellow showing through the dirt.

'My,' said Mr MacPherson, 'I do believe— I really do believe—yes—it's Mamie and Semolina! However did you get so dirty?'

Mamie and Semolina hung their heads.

'I suppose you've been in the orchard,' said Mr MacPherson sternly. 'But I don't think you'll ever want to go in the orchard again.'

Then Mr MacPherson went inside and brought out a bowl of warm water, and he shook a lot of soap flakes into it, and when it was all frothed up nicely he put Mamie and Semolina in the bowl. They looked so funny sticking up out of the white froth that Mr

MacPherson had to laugh. Then he scrubbed them with a brush till they were clean again, and then he carried them, one under each arm, down to the dam and rinsed them.

Then he gave them some mash for their tea and they began to feel better. It is not a nice feeling to be sticky and dirty all over.

Mamie and Semolina often swam in the dam or played in the long grass with the other ducks, but they never went in the orchard again.

And every day they each laid a big white egg for Mr MacPherson.

From *Storytime* by Marjorie Cleine

Mrs Peck Pigeon

Mrs Peck Pigeon
  Is picking for bread;
Bob, bob, bob,
  Goes her little round head.

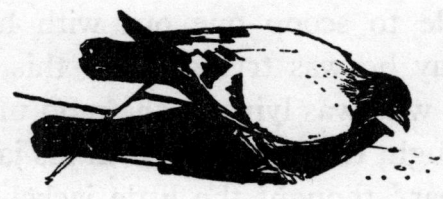

Tame as a pussy cat
  In the street,
Step, step, step,
  Go her little red feet,

With her little red feet
  And her little round head
Mrs Peck Pigeon
  Goes picking for bread.

From *Silver Sand and Snow*
by Eleanor Farjeon

The Jackal and the Crocodile

THE jackal is very fond of eating crabs. He finds them along the edge of the river and although he can't catch them in the water, sometimes he is able to scoop one out with his paw.

One day he was trying to do this when a crocodile who was lying in the mud under the water, caught the jackal's paw in his jaws.

'Oh dear,' thought the little jackal. 'Whatever shall I do? How can I escape?'

Then he had a good idea. He called out loudly so that the crocodile would hear, 'You're too clever, Mr Crocodile! That's not my paw —it's the root of a tree you've got in your mouth.'

As he was under the mud, the crocodile believed the cunning jackal and let his paw go.

Away ran the little jackal, laughing, and as he ran he sang:

> 'I'm clever, clever, clever!
> You'll never catch me—never!'

which made the crocodile very angry, but there wasn't anything he could do about it.

The jackal didn't have crab for dinner for several days, but one day he felt he must have one again, so he went back to the river.

There was no sign of the crocodile, but the jackal knew he must be more careful this time. So he said loudly, so that the crocodile would hear him, 'I don't see any crabs sticking up out of the water today. There can't be any about, I suppose. I'd better go home again.'

The crocodile heard what the jackal said and he thought, 'If I stick my nose up above the water, the jackal will think it is a crab and will try to catch it. Then I can catch *him* and eat him for my dinner.'

So he stuck his big nose out of the water, but directly the jackal saw it he knew the crocodile was there, and he ran away singing:

> 'I'm clever, clever, clever!
> You'll never catch me—never!'

For some time the jackal had no crabs for dinner, but one day he woke up feeling that he must have one that very day. So he went down to the river again. There was not a crab to be seen along the bank and he was afraid to put his paw into the water. So he said in a loud voice, 'Now I wonder if there are any crabs today? If there are, I shall see them blowing bubbles—bubble, plop, bubble, plop—then I shall be able to catch them.'

The crocodile was down in the mud but he heard what the jackal said. 'Ah, ha!' he thought. '*I'll* blow bubbles and then the jackal will put his paw in the water and I shall catch him at last.'

So he took a deep breath and blew. Instead of small bubbles, the water shot up like a fountain! In fact he blew so hard that a little crab was lifted right out of the river and fell at the jackal's feet.

'Ha, ha!' laughed the little jackal as he snapped up the crab:

'I'm clever, clever, clever!
You'll never catch me—NEVER!'

And away he ran.

The crocodile was so angry that he dragged himself out of the water and tried to run after the jackal, but of course he couldn't catch him.

So he sank back into the mud again, while far away the jackal laughed and sang mockingly:

'. . . clever, clever, clever!
You'll never catch me—never!'

              Traditional, adapted by Eileen Colwell

If You Find a Little Feather

If you find a little feather,
A little white feather,
A soft and tickly feather,
  it's for you.

A feather is a letter
from a bird,
and it says,
'Think of me,
Remember me always.
Remember me for ever.
Oh remember me
at least
until
the little feather
is
lost!'

So . . . if you find a little feather,
A little white feather,
A soft and tickly feather,
   it's for you.
Pick it up and . . .
put it in your pocket.

From *Something Special*
by Beatrice Schenck de Regniers

All Change!

THERE were once four friends. They were a small ginger kitten, a small white puppy, a little brown rabbit, and a baby rook. They lived in the country and they had all sorts of fun together. Sometimes Baby Rook used to pick off tiny twigs and fir cones and drop them down from his home high up in the trees for Kitten to play with. Sometimes Puppy would roll his rubber ball right down Rabbit's hole for Rabbit to play with. Sometimes Rabbit would pick a dandelion clock from the meadow and send the little white fluffets puffing up and up for Baby Rook to catch. Sometimes Kitten would hold her old cotton reel on a string in her sharp white teeth and let Puppy chase it round the garden. They were always thinking of new tricks to play and new things to do. And then, one day, when they had played all their old games a hundred times and were sitting round thinking of something quite new to do, Kitten had a great idea.

'I know,' she cried. 'Let's all change houses for one night!'

'Change houses?' squawked Baby Rook.

'Change houses?' snuffled Rabbit.

'Change houses?' woofed Puppy.

Then they all cried together, 'What *do* you mean, Kitten?'

The small ginger kitten looked at them and she said, 'I mean, why shouldn't we all try living in one another's houses? Just for a change, of course, not for ever. I'm a good climber so I'd better go up in Rook's high tree.'

'And I'm a good burrower,' said Puppy, 'so I could have a turn in Rabbit's home.'

'I couldn't bear to be shut up indoors,' said Baby Rook, 'so I'd better go in Puppy's box in the stable.'

'And that means I can sleep in Kitten's cosy basket by the fire,' said the little brown rabbit. 'What fun!'

As soon as they saw the sun was setting ready for bed the four little friends all thought they had better begin to settle into their new homes for the night.

Kitten looked up and up the high tree where Baby Rook's nest was tucked in between some twigs, and she wasn't so sure she wanted to sleep there after all. But she didn't like to say co because the others might think she was a sowardly cat. So she called, 'Good night!' dug her sharp claws into the rough bark of the tree, and began to climb.

Puppy looked down Rabbit's dark hole and he wasn't so sure he wanted to sleep there after all. But he didn't want the others to think he was afraid, so he called, 'Good night!' and crept into the dark passage that went on and on and out of sight.

Baby Rook fluttered along to the stable where Puppy slept in a box full of straw on the ground. It looked very low down and she thought it might be very dangerous if people should want to tread there. She wasn't so sure she wanted to sleep there after all. But all the others were going to their new homes and she wasn't going to be the only one left out, so she cawed 'Good night!' and hopped into the stable.

The little brown rabbit was left alone. He scuttled over to the back door and poked his head round. There inside, by the fire, was Kitten's basket with a soft cushion in it and a saucer of milk nearby. He didn't much like the idea of having no nice dark corner to huddle in, but he had nowhere else to sleep now, so in he went, plip-plop, plip-plop!

By the time Kitten had scrambled and clawed her way right up to Rook's home, she was quite worn out. It felt very wobbly and chilly high up there in the tree, but she was too tired to care any more and she curled round and tried to go to sleep.

By the time Puppy had scrambled and bumped his way all along the stuffy dark passages to Rabbit's home, he was quite worn out. It felt damp and chilly under the ground, but he was too tired to care any more and he flopped down and tried to go to sleep.

By the time Baby Rook had poked and twisted the straw in Puppy's box into some sort of hollow to snuggle into, she was quite worn out. It felt dusty and hard in the box but she was too tired to care any more. She tucked her head down and tried to go to sleep.

By the time Rabbit had turned the cushion in Kitten's basket this way and that and poked his head underneath to try to shut out the light from the fire, he was quite worn out. It felt hot and stuffy in the kitchen and he kept hearing strange noises that upset him, but he was really too tired to care any more and he burrowed in as best he could and tried to go to sleep.

Presently the wind arose and the rain began to fall.

Baby Rook's nest swayed to and fro, high up in the tree. Kitten was very frightened. 'MIAOU! I'm not staying up here,' she said to herself and she began to hurry down to the ground again.

The rain grew heavier and heavier. Little cold streams of water trickled down Rabbit's passage and made puddles on the earth floor. Puppy was shivering and miserable. 'OO-OW!' he howled sadly. 'I'm not staying here any more.' And he hurried down the passage to get above ground again.

The wind blew stronger and louder. The stable door creaked and squeaked and began to bang to and fro. Baby Rook was frightened.

'CAA-CAA!' she squawked. 'I'm not staying here. I might get shut in for ever.' And she flew out as fast as she could.

Inside by the fire it was warm enough and Rabbit didn't even know there was a storm blowing. But the fire crackled and spat and a cinder fell out near his fluffy coat. Rabbit was frightened. 'POOFF! I'm not staying here,' he said to himself. 'I might catch fire!' And he scuttled off as fast as he could go.

In a few minutes the storm was over and a big golden moon came shining out of the clouds. It shone down on the garden and the fields and what did it see? One small ginger kitten, one small white puppy, one little brown rabbit, and one baby rook, all looking very lost and scared and all so surprised to see each other. And it wasn't long, I can tell you, before Kitten was curled up cosily in her basket; Puppy was snuggled down in his box of straw; little brown Rabbit was safely underground in his burrow; and Baby Rook was swaying peacefully away high up in her tree-top.

And not one of them ever suggested playing the 'All Change' game again!

From *Country Bunch* by Ursula Hourihane

Good-Night

Now good-night.
Fold up your clothes
As you were taught,
Fold your two hands,
Fold up your thought;
Day is the plough-land,
Night is the stream,
Day is for doing
And night is the dream.
Now good-night.

From *Silver Sand and Snow*
by Eleanor Farjeon

Baboushka

LONG, long ago, an old woman, Baboushka, lived all alone in a little hut in the forest. One night of snow and bitter cold, she heard footsteps outside her hut. Several people were drawing near, the frozen snow crackling under their feet. Who could be travelling so late at night through the dark forest? Surely all good men should be indoors.

There came a knock at the door. 'Who are you?' called the old woman fearfully.

'Do not be afraid. We are travellers from a far country. We wish only to ask our way.' And hearing the kindness in the stranger's voice, Baboushka knew that there was nothing to fear.

She opened the door. Outside the snow was falling thick and fast. In the snow stood three tall men.

'Come in,' said Baboushka shivering. 'You must be cold and hungry. Rest for a while.'

'We must not stay,' said the strangers, 'but we will step inside the better to ask our question.' The three men came into the small warm room with its glowing stove and flickering candlelight.

The old woman saw that her visitors were dressed in rich robes of a kind she had never seen before, and were of different races. They bore themselves so proudly that it seemed to her that they must be kings in their own land.

Said the first stranger: 'We have travelled far, following a bright Star. Now the sky is hidden by the falling snow and we have lost our way.'

Said the second stranger: 'When we have found the Star again, we shall follow it to a place where a baby has been born.'

Said the third stranger: 'And this baby is born to be King of the World.'

'I have seen no star,' said Baboushka, 'and I have heard of no King. I am but a poor woman. Rest here, good sirs.'

'We must be on our way. Will you not come with us to find the baby who is to be King?' asked the strangers.

'It is too cold,' said the old woman. 'I am too busy. I will come tomorrow perhaps.'

'Tomorrow may be too late,' said the first stranger, opening the door. One by one the three kingly travellers stepped out into the driving snow and disappeared.

Baboushka closed the door and sat by the warm stove to drink her tea. But she was not happy.

'I should have gone with them,' she thought. 'I might have been able to help them to find their way. I should have liked to see that baby. I will go—in the morning.'

Early next morning she put some small gifts such as children love into a bag and set out. But the drifting snow had covered the strangers' footsteps. There was nothing to show her which way the Kings had gone.

Of everyone she met, she asked, 'Have you seen three Kings pass by?'

'Kings!' they exclaimed. 'How should we have seen Kings?'

'Have you seen the Star, then?' she asked.

The people laughed. 'Everyone has seen stars,' they said. 'They all look much alike.'

'Has a baby been born in these parts? A baby born to be King?' asked Baboushka.

'Babies are born every day,' the people said. 'No baby born here will ever become a King.'

Carrying her bag the old woman walked on and on. Days, weeks, months went by, but she

found no baby or star and saw no Kings. But she met many children who were hungry and unhappy and, whenever she could, she gave to each a gift from her bag so that their tears changed to smiles.

And although this happened so long, long ago, some people say that old Baboushka still travels the world at Christmas time carrying gifts for the children and bringing happiness wherever she goes.

Traditional, retold by Eileen Colwell

The Little Fir-Tree

THE earth was white, covered with the fine feathery mantle thrown down from the sky. The grass and trees felt warm under the snow. In the wood every dark branch was outlined with silver, and every holly leaf held a bunch of snowflakes in its hollow green cup. The great beeches spread out their bare boughs and caught the snow in the net of twigs, and the birches stood like frozen fountains, very beautiful.

Near the edge of the wood was a plantation of fir-trees, all very young and small. Their dark outstretched skirts were soon white, so that each tree looked like a little shining umbrella. Now one tree was different from the others, for it possessed a treasure which it held tightly to its heart. It was a nest, which had been built in the spring by a speckled thrush. It was so neat and trim that the fir-tree was very proud of it, and sheltered it with its close thick branches so that no snow fell on it.

The little fir-tree had loved the singing bird which lived there. It had taken care of the eggs and guarded the nestlings from owls and robbers till they were old enough to fly away. It had listened to the thrush's song, and moved its slender branches to the music. When the birds went, the tree waited for them to return or for another bird to come to the empty nest, but the rain fell, and the winds blew, and no bird sat in the home hidden in the heart of the tree.

'Perhaps a winter bird will come, a dazzling white bird, and it will lay eggs of ivory and pearl in my nest,' said the little fir-tree when it saw the snow, but the other trees round it shook their heads till the snow fell in a shower.

'Only hens could do that,' said they, 'and they stay in the farmyards this wintry weather. There will be no bird till next year.'

Then they drooped their branches and waited patiently till they were completely covered up again by the warm white blanket.

In a cottage down the lane lived a little boy and girl. They made a fine snowman outside their kitchen window, and stuck an old broken pipe of their grandfather's in its wide mouth, and a stick in its hand. They pulled each other up and down the fields in a wooden box, pretending it was a sledge drawn by a pair of fine horses. They made a long slide in the lane, and glided along it, with arms outstretched to the cold air, pretending they were flying birds. They looked at the icy frost-ferns on the windows of the little rooms under the thatched roof, and called them 'Jack Frost's Garden'.

'The children at the Castle are going to have a Christmas tree,' said Peter, pushing his wet red hand into his mother's.

'And it's going to be all a-dazzle with lights and things,' said Sarah.

'Such things are not for us. They cost too much money, but you are going to have a pair of boots apiece, and that's more useful. Maybe Santa Claus will put something in your stocking, too, if you've been good.' Their mother sighed, knowing how hard it was to manage. She packed them off early to bed, but the grandfather nodded his head and smiled to himself.

On Christmas Eve the old man came into the wood, carrying a spade. He hunted here and there looking at this tree and that, peering at the colony of firs like a wise owl that wants to find a home. One tree was too big, another too scraggy, another too bushy. Then he saw the little fir-tree, standing like a fairy on one leg, wearing a crinoline of snowy crystals.

'That's the tree! That's the tree for me! Not too big, and not too little, with plenty of close branches, as smooth and round as a bell,' he cried aloud, for, like many old people, he had a habit of speaking to himself for company.

He shook the snow from the twigs with tender old fingers and then dug round the tree, gathering all the fibrous roots carefully in his hands.

'Oh dear me!' cried the little fir-tree. 'What is going to happen? Do be careful, old man. Don't shake the nest out of my branches!' The sound of its voice was like a sobbing breeze, and the other trees shook their heads and waved their tiny boughs mournfully.

'Goodbye,' they called. 'Goodbye for ever.'

'Whatever happens, I am glad. It's a great adventure,' the little fir-tree sang out bravely, when the old man carried it away.

Across the fields and along the lane it went in the old grandfather's warm hands, and the tall trees in the hedgerows looked with pity at it. Little rabbits peeped round the corners of the walls, and a hare stared through a gap to see who was singing the song of the woods. When they saw the fir-tree they nodded and whispered, 'Poor thing! He's caught in a trap!' and they scurried away.

The grandfather walked through a wooden gate, and up the garden path to the cottage door. Then he put the tree in the wood-shed till the children went to bed. He wiped his spade, washed his hands and sat down to tea without saying anything.

At last it was bedtime, and Peter and Sarah had their baths on the kitchen hearth, where a great fire blazed, and sparks flew up the chimney. They sat on their stools and ate their bread and milk, and a mince-pie because it was Christmas Eve. Then they each took a candle and trundled up the crooked stair to their little beds, but just as they kissed good-night to their mother and grandfather, Peter lifted his head and listened.

'I can hear a little singing noise,' said he. 'What is it?'

Sarah listened too. 'It's only the wind in the woodshed,' she told her brother, and she ran to tie her stocking to the bedpost, ready for Santa Claus.

When all was quiet upstairs, the grandfather

fetched the little tree into the house. The fire crackled, and the tree began to tremble with the heat, so that the twigs rustled and its song died away with fright. 'This is the end,' it thought.

'Here's a little tiddly Christmas tree for Peter and Sarah,' said the old man. 'But take great care of it, for I must put it back in the wood where I found it.'

The mother dropped her sewing and smiled at her father. 'Oh, Grandfather! What a surprise! What a perfect little tree!'

She gazed at the green tree, with its shining branches, to which a powder of snow still clung. There was something particularly beautiful about the tree, fresh from its dreams in the wood. As for the little fir-tree, it plucked up courage and stared round at the room, at the table with the bread and cheese, and the cat on the hearth, and the china dogs on the mantelpiece, and the holly wreath over the loud-ticking clock.

'There's a nest in it,' went on the grandfather, proudly, 'Peter will like that,' and he showed the mother the neat round nest hidden under the branches.

'Now I'm going out to buy some things to

hang on it, so that it will be as fine as the tree up at the Castle. You plant it carefully all ready for me!' He reached up to the teapot on the mantelpiece, the lustre teapot which was his moneybox, and took out some coins.

'I'm going to be extravagant for once, for I've got a bit of my pension left,' he laughed, and he set off down the dark lanes to the village shop.

While he was away, the mother planted the tree in plenty of soil in the big earthenware breadmug which stood in the corner of the room, stocked with her home-made loaves. The bread she placed in a row on the dresser, small round cobs, each with a cross on the top in memory of the Christ child, and the tree she dragged to the middle of the room, near the lamp and her sewing. As her needle went in and out she heard a tiny singing sound, and she knew it was the happy tree chanting its woodland song.

After some time the old man came back with a brown-paper parcel and bulging pockets. From the parcel he took little red and blue and gold balls to hang on the tree, and a silver glass trumpet, and four tiny coloured glass bells with little clappers which tinkled like icicles. He had a box of silver tinsel tassels to droop from the boughs like falling water, and a couple of golden roses. He brought from his pockets two oranges, and three rosy apples, and a couple of tiny baskets of almond fruits. The mother and the old man hung them all about the tree so that it looked as if the little glossy fir-tree had stepped straight out of fairyland.

On the tip-top of the tree's head, the grandfather's shaking fingers fastened a little Dutch doll with a wisp of tinsel round her waist, a midget of a doll as big as his thumb-nail, and in the nest he placed a lovely glass bird, with a white body and feathery tail and a silver beak and wings.

The tree quivered with delight, so that all the bells began to ring, and all the balls and sparkles jumped up and down and gleamed in the firelight. At last a bird had come to live in the nest again, a winter bird, snow-white like the frosty earth!

Throughout Christmas Eve the tree stayed in the quiet room, listening to the ticking of the clock, and the chink, chink of the dying fire, and the chirrup of the cricket which lived under the hearthstone, and the tree, too, murmured and rustled its branches, waiting for the glass bird to chirp and sing.

Then dawn came, and the mother made the fire again, so that the lights sprang out and the tree's dark branches reflected the glow. The kettle sang, the blue cups and saucers were placed with their tinkling spoons on the clean white cloth, and the bacon hissed in the frying-pan.

Suddenly there was a patter of feet, and a sound of laughter on the stairs. The door burst open and the two children came running in, carrying bulging little stockings in their hands.

'A Merry Christmas! A Merry Christmas!' they cried, hugging their mother and grandfather. Then they saw the pretty tree standing as demure as a little girl in her first party frock, and they gave a shout.

'A Christmas tree! Where did it come from? Oh! How lovely! It's a real live one, growing.'

'There's a teeny, tiny doll on the top. Is it for me?' asked Sarah.

'There's a real nest,' exclaimed Peter, 'and there's a bird in it, too.' They both danced round the tree singing:

'Christmas comes but once a year,
And when it comes it brings good cheer.'

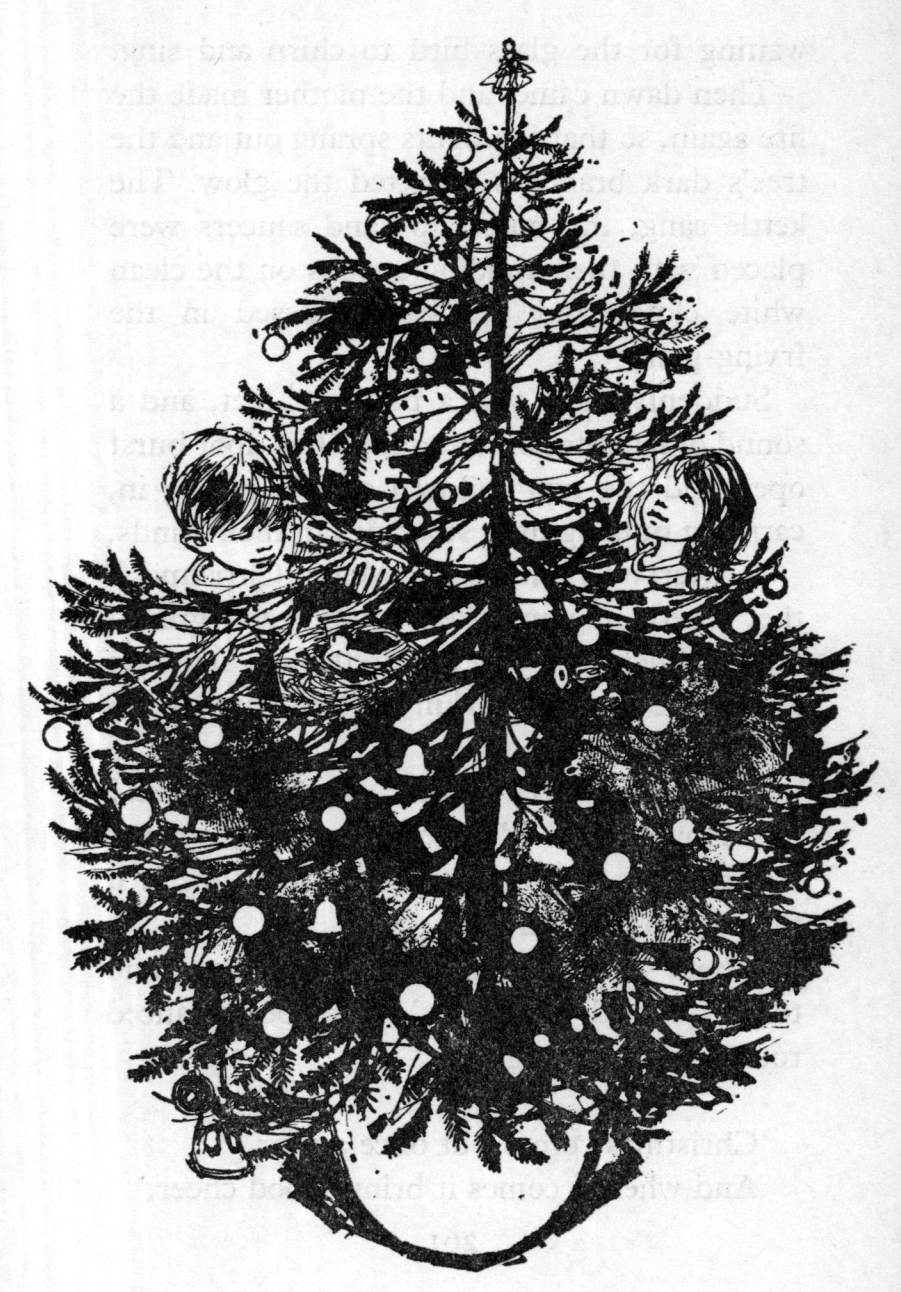

'Just see if that bird has laid any eggs,' said the smiling old grandfather, and when Peter slipped his hand in the thrush's nest he found two silver sixpences!

That was a day for the fir-tree to remember! Never as long as it lived would it forget that day! It stood, the centre of the festivities, watching the Christmas games, listening to the Christmas songs, humming softly to the bells from the church across the village green.

'Can't you hear it?' whispered Peter. 'The tree is singing.' But Sarah said it was only the wind through the keyhole, for trees never sang.

In a few days the grandfather took the fir-tree back to the wood, with the nest safe and sound under the branches. He uncovered the hole, and planted the roots deep in it, so that the tree stood firmly among its companions.

'Tell us again,' cried the fir-trees in the plantation, when the little tree had told its story for the hundredth time. 'Did you say a snow-white bird came to live in your nest? Did you have bells on your boughs? And gold roses? Tell us again.'

So once more the fir-tree told the story of Christmas.

'But the bird never sang at all,' it added. 'I

shall be glad to see my thrush again next spring. The bells were not as sweet-sounding as the bluebells in the wood, and the roses had no scent at all. But it was a beautiful Christmas, and I was very, very happy!'

From *The Weathercock and Other Stories* by Alison Uttley

FOR THE STORYTELLER

For the Storyteller

I was asked to make this collection of stories as a direct result of the popularity of my two previous anthologies. The parents, teachers and librarians who have used my other books have felt the need for a similar collection of stories for the youngest children.

Anyone who has had experience of working with little children will know how insatiable is their demand for stories. Unable to read for themselves, they rely on adults to satisfy this need. Restricted to the small world of their own experience, it is mainly through stories that their imagination develops.

The technique of telling stories to these young children must of necessity vary from that used with older children who have already learnt to concentrate and to read for themselves. Many parents make the mistake of expecting the child to listen attentively to too long a story, forgetting that the young child's span of concentration is very brief, probably no more than ten minutes at the most.

With a child at your knee who is probably well known to you, the story can be selected and adapted to suit his taste, and time can be taken to explain difficult or unfamiliar details. Most children look forward to the bedtime story but mothers realise that this should be carefully chosen so as not to excite the child unduly. No story in this book will give a child nightmares!

A story hour for a *group* of children needs a different approach. The storyteller must be able to recognise signs of inattention and to understand why they are happening. It may be that the story is too long or that something has been introduced that is so far outside the child's experience that it is incomprehensible to him. Or perhaps the storyteller is talking too quickly. A break at the conclusion of the story may be advisable so that the children can move energetically, chant nursery rhymes or participate in some simple activity such as finger plays. (A good source for these is *This Little Pig went to Market*, compiled by Norah Montgomerie.)

The inexperienced storyteller will often be disconcerted by a child's apparently irrelevant comments. These may not be as irrelevant as they appear for probably some chance reference in the story has reminded the child of something that is important to him—a new pair of shoes, for instance. The storyteller can sometimes weave this interruption into her story, but the child's remark should never be ignored or it will be repeated again and again until it gains attention. The storyteller must remain in control if the interest of the children is to be kept.

No matter how simple the story, it can have drama and characterisation, surprise and suspense, and the storyteller can enhance these attractions by the tone of her voice and the use of pauses and a varying pace in telling.

What kind of stories do children under school age enjoy? Picture books are loved by every child and are essential to his development, but they are not my concern here. Most story books for this age are well illustrated, as is this one. Young children enjoy stories of familiar things and happenings linked to their everyday experience, stories of animals and birds, and the simpler traditional tales such as *The Three Bears*. Machines and toys that talk are favourite themes, for it is natural for the child to think of everything around him as having personality. How often have we heard children talking to their toys and acting out stories of their mutual adventures!

A story in which there is repetition is always a favourite.

Simple repetitive phrases are soon learnt and the children join eagerly in

'Run, run, as fast as you can
You can't catch me—I'm the Gingerbread Man.'

or the recurring jingle in the story *Sleepy-Mouse* in this book. The child loves funny stories, although his sense of humour may be very elementary. Even a sneeze is intensely amusing to him and he will join with gusto in Tim Rabbit's 'Atishoo!' The thought of Jacko the monkey wearing a potato scone on his head and sitting on another one, is both funny and satisfying, for how often the child himself has wanted to be naughty like this and has been prevented. Vicarious naughtiness is always enjoyed. Animal noises are another excuse for joining in actively and are provided with great enthusiasm, expecially a pig's grunt. The urge to participate is both enjoyable for the child and useful to the storyteller as a means of holding attention and using a child's natural energy.

The homely story of their own childhood told by grandparents or other relatives, always appeals. It has the added attraction that it happened to someone the child loves and trusts and it is true.

There is so much in the everyday world around him to arouse the child's wonder and this, seen through the eyes of a poet, gives the child a joyous experience. There are many poems with simple images and a rhythmic pattern and music which even the youngest child can appreciate.

Simplicity, but not sentimentality or under-estimation of a child's intelligence, is the keynote of all storytelling for little children. To share a story or poem with them is a delightful and rewarding experience.

EILEEN COLWELL